The
Rainbow Quest of

THOMAS
PYNCHON

Douglas A. Mackey

R. Reginald

THE 𝕭𝖔𝖗𝖌𝖔 𝕻𝖗𝖊𝖘𝖘

San Bernardino, California

MCMLXXX

For Laurie, who made this possible

Thanks to Heather and Wayne Hall
and to Douglas Taylor
for reviewing the manuscript.

Library of Congress Cataloging in Publication Data:

Mackey, Douglas A   1947-
    The rainbow quest of Thomas Pynchon.

    (The Milford Series: Popular Writers of Today ; v. 28) (ISSN 0163-2469)
    Bibliography: p. 62-63.
    1. Pynchon, Thomas—Criticism and interpretation. I. Title.
PS3566.Y55Z69   813'.54   80-11219
ISBN 0-89370-142-4 (Cloth edition; $8.95)
ISBN 0-89370-242-0 (Paper edition; $2.95)

Produced, designed, and published by R. Reginald, The Borgo Press, P.O. Box 2845, San Bernardino, CA 92406, USA. Composition and paste-up by Irene Frost. Cover design by Judy Cloyd Graphic Design.

First Edition————June, 1980

Chapter One
FROM HERE TO ENTROPY

What if we were to start noticing cryptic clues in our lives, subtle indicators that beneath the mundane and random daily events there was a carefully planned pattern engineered by somebody or something? What if we began to believe that the world as we ordinarily experience it—in newspapers and on television, in conversations with friends, in the familiar solidity of our home and work environments—was a sham, an illusion that concealed plots, organizations, conspiracies? What if we suspected that our own minds had been programmed to play a film of delusory sensory phenomena to a captive audience of one, while somewhere else *real* life was going on?

The characters in Thomas Pynchon's novels are obsessed with questions like these. They are paranoids and have good reason to be. They quest for a transcendent meaning in a chaotic world whose energy seems to be running down; but the more they find out about the conspiracies the less they know, and they finally end in complete indeterminacy. The reader is unsatisfied: the mystery does not resolve itself neatly like a whodunit—it multiplies. And the only remedy for this sense of uncertainty and disorientation is—to read more Pynchon.

There must be a cabal of Pynchon adepts, like the Tristero in his second novel, *The Crying of Lot 49*. It is logical that such a secret society would exist, with its hierophants, codes, signs, ceremonies, and plots. Perhaps all those of us who read Pynchon—and get hooked on whatever it is he is trying to tell us—are unofficial members of the society.

These facts are known about Pynchon: he was born in 1943 on Long Island, attended Cornell University, studied engineering and physics while majoring in English, served a hitch in the Navy, was a close friend of Richard Farina, and worked as an engineering aide for Boeing in Seattle for a couple of years while writing *V.*, his first novel. Since it was published, his profile has diminished from low to non-existent. There are no known photographs of him; his whereabouts are unknown; he does not make talk show appearances, give readings on campuses, or submit to interviews in literary magazines. He prefers to let his work speak for him.

Pynchon's three novels—*V.* (1963), *The Crying of Lot 49* (1966), and *Gravity's Rainbow* (1973)—have attained a measure of popular success, but also earned him a reputation as a "difficult" author. Because the academic establishment thrives on difficulty, books and articles about him and his work have proliferated. Perhaps more has been written on Pynchon than on any other contemporary American author, and the effect of reading this considerable body of criticism is not always inspiriting to someone who wants to "understand" the writer. The explanations often seem more complicated than the novels themselves. But the attempt is not ignoble, and after all, members of a cabal must communicate.

Critics often cite the following as blocks to comprehension or appreciation: encyclopedic detail, themes and metaphors based on physics, engineering, and calculus; manic humor, often of the lowest farcical variety; incessant satire of corporate institutions, the media, and the counterculture; obscenity; cardboard characters with impossible names; lack of distinction between fantasy and reality; improbable songs stuck in for cheap laughs; put-ons of the reader by the narrator. All of these are true, and all are virtues. But there is another dimension to Pynchon that is not as well-recognized by most critics, and that is the poetry of his language. Amidst the frenetic activity of his plots, there are spaces for repose, contemplation, dreams. "Only at moments of great serenity is it possible to find the pure, the informationless state of signal zero," says Pynchon in *Gravity's Rainbow* (p.470; all page references are to the Bantam paperback editions of Pynchon's novels). Through his lyrical passages he induces that state—a kind of floating, euphoric equilibrium.

Here, for example, from *Gravity's Rainbow*, is the description of how Big Ben must be speeded up at night in order to compensate for war-time drains on the electricity reserves: "In the night, the deepest concrete wells of night, dynamos whose locations are classified spin faster, and so, responding, the clock-hands next to all the old, sleepless eyes—gathering in their minutes whining, pitching higher toward the vertigo of a siren. It is the Night's Mad Carnival. There is merriment under the shadows of the minute-hands. Hysteria in the pale faces between the numerals. . .and the numbers go whirling toward the Nativity, a violence, a nova of heart that will turn us all, change us forever to the very forgotten roots of who we are. But over the sea the fog tonight still is quietly scalloped pearl. Up in the city the arc-lamps crackle, furious, in smothered blaze up the centerlines of the streets, too ice-colored for candles, too chill-dropleted for holocaust. . ." (p.156).

The contrast between forces of violent change and those of peace and silence creates the equilibrium of signal zero, a state of infinite receptivity to all possibilities. The surge of the dynamos on Christmas Eve propels the clock towards Nativity, a spiritual rebirth evoked movingly by the image of "quietly scalloped pearl." This sort of poetry is always drifting through Pynchon's cosmos, crystalline visionary glimpses breaking through the darkness of terror, silence cutting off the noise of gross laughter.

There is poetry too in Pynchon's frequent catalogues of the trivial minutiae of everyday life, as in this list from *The Crying of Lot 49* of junk found in used car trade-ins: ". . .clipped coupons promising savings of 5 or 10¢, trading stamps, pink flyers advertising specials at the markets, butts, tooth-shy combs, help-wanted ads, Yellow Pages torn from the phone book, rags of old underwear or dresses that already were period costumes, for wiping your own breath off the inside of a windshield with so you could see whatever it was, a movie, a woman or car you coveted, a cop who might pull you over just for drill, all the bits and pieces coated uniformly, like a salad of despair, in a gray dressing of ash, condensed exhaust, dust, body wastes. . ." (p.5). The inevitability of these items is wonderful. They may seem like images randomly piled, but every detail reinforces the inner coherency of this "salad of despair." Pynchon's poetry of accumulation adds greatly to the force of his purposes, be they comic, tragic, or moral.

It has been thought by some critics that Pynchon's characters are not very "realistic" or engaging. That is a matter of perception. Fantastical as they may be, they are nevertheless believable. They are morally neither black nor white as a rule; in fact, Pynchon can elicit more compassion for his supposed villains, such as Blicero and V., than for his picaresque heroes, such as Benny Profane and Tyrone Slothrop. Pynchon's characters often have as much psychological ambiguity as we could desire from the most naturalistic of writers. On the surface these characters seem more like caricatures, but appearances are deceiving. For example, if we read *Gravity's Rainbow* on only one level, Tyrone Slothrop is a man without introspection. His main concern is to ingest as many drugs and inoculate as many women with his sperm as possible. He has no great ideas, no stirring emotions. But strangely, through his emotional passivity, it becomes possible for us to enter into his experience and feel its humor and pathos. Slothrop's neutrality promotes our identification with him; no strong character ego blocks our empathy. The character does not live as do those in the novels of Virginia Woolf or James Joyce, where thoughts are accessible to scrutiny, and arrange themselves in subtle waves that give the illusion of reality. Slothrop lives insofar as we, the readers, animate him. We care about him because he is an innocent, and so are we at heart.

The much-vaunted "difficulty" of reading Pynchon's novels is due more to the density of his language than to the obscurity of his mathematical or philosophical references. As when reading Joyce, we do not expect to understand everything. It is also true that Pynchon, like Joyce, requires rereading for anything approximating comprehension. This is particularly true of *Gravity's Rainbow*. His first two novels are more accessible. *The Crying of Lot 49* is a very short book—very dense, it is true—but a good starting place. It has a straightforward narrative time frame, one central character, and a main plot; its satire of Southern California culture is direct and very funny. This novel is a marvel of simplicity that conceals a network of complex meanings, images, and themes beneath its surface. Undervalued when it first appeared, it has surpassed *V.* in critical estimation because of the fresh insights that repeated readings make possible.

Superficially, *V.* is more difficult in its structure—it jumps around from past to present; details necessary to understanding one part of the book may be hidden in another—but it is not as complex in underlying meaning as *Lot 49*. Its secrets are reasonably accessible, but it should be approached in the spirit of a game in which the author will sometimes intentionally

5

frustrate the reader, making certain details obscure so that he will have to stop and say "Wha," like Benny Profane in the novel is wont to do. *V.* is arguably the funniest of Pynchon's books, if only because those lovable degenerates, the Whole Sick Crew, are so cleverly etched, as if they had stepped out of a Moliere farce like personifications of the Humours, gorged to excess with phlegm or blood or bile.

Gravity's Rainbow is Pynchon's masterpiece. With its nine hundred pages and four hundred characters, it is a formidable mountain for any reader to attempt. At first it may seem chaotic, a huge accretion of verbal debris, a kind of dumping ground where Pynchon has deposited bits of mathematics, history, bawdy limericks, poetry, pornography, physics, film, theosophy, philosophy, and the sounds of wisecracks, doper's slang, blues, and kazoos. In his essay "Gravity's Encyclopedia" (in *Mindful Pleasures: Essays on Thomas Pynchon*), Edward Mendelson places it in the genre of encyclopedic narrative along with Dante's *Divine Comedy*, Rabelais's *Gargantua and Pantagruel*, Cervantes's *Don Quixote*, Goethe's *Faust*, Melville's *Moby Dick*, and Joyce's *Ulysses*. It certainly rivals the latter in difficulty and shares with all of these the presentation of a mass of information about the culture from which it springs. A list of recommended reading to illuminate Pynchon's wealth of recurrent allusions and themes might include Ludwig Wittgenstein, Werner Heisenberg, Max Weber, Goethe, Norbert Wiener, Rainer Maria Rilke, Richard Wagner, Alfred North Whitehead, works on the history of science, introductory calculus texts, and perhaps some superhero comic books. *Gravity's Rainbow* casts its nets outward into the world. It stuns us with its sheer quantity of reference, and forces us to explore, integrate, and hypothesize outside the sphere of the novel itself. We should expect to be overwhelmed. But the complexity here is of a different order than in *V.* and *Lot 49*: it defies reduction because the sum of its parts is so vast we don't even have a chance to compare it to the whole.

Gravity's Rainbow is unclassifiable. Ostensibly about World War II, it juxtaposes sobering frames from the darkest years of the century with flamboyant fantasy that makes it float free of historical reference. It was nominated for the Nebula Award for best science fiction novel of the year; it missed the prize, perhaps because some felt it didn't fit the category. Indeed, it encompasses that category and many others: historical novel, mystery, satire, love story, absurdist novel, comic book, travelogue, songbook. It contains multitudes. Although *The Crying of Lot 49* is perfect in its economy of symbol and taut narrative line, and *V.* is expansive, richly humorous, a captivating puzzle, *Gravity's Rainbow* takes Pynchon's art into a new, more ambitious dimension.

As a preface to a discussion of the three novels, we shall take a look at several short stories and an article published early in Pynchon's career. His first major published story was "Mortality and Mercy in Vienna" (1959), in which a wild party terminates abruptly when a melancholic Ojibwa Indian, Irving Loon, succumbs to what is known as the "Windigo psychosis" and peppers the guests with an automatic rifle. That is the "mortality." The "mercy" is purely ironic, for Cleanth Siegel, who has been thrust unwillingly into the host's role, enjoys the feeling of control as he allows the massacre to occur, as though it were an act of mercy to put the decadent assemblage out of its misery.

Siegel is a successful junior diplomat who had in college "instigated protest riots and panty raids, manipulated campus opinion through the school newspaper." There is little in this clean-cut image to suggest an accomplice in a mass-murder save perhaps his eagerness to get the upper hand over others, and his being "not particularly aware of destruction"— ignorant, that is, of his own destructive potential. He arrives for the party at the apartment of one David Lupescu, a wild-eyed Rumanian who styles himself after Kurtz in Conrad's *Heart of Darkness*, a civilized man who becomes debased in his jungle outpost, and who in this case serves as a father-confessor to a bohemian crowd. Siegel senses a doppelganger relationship between Lupescu and himself: they are spiritual doubles; and feeling this also, the impulsive Lupescu gets Siegel to replace him as host to the arriving guests.

Siegel listens to the amatory traumas of a couple of the women, and absolves them as Lupescu would have done; but he possesses little capacity for self-reflection. He does, however, have sufficient pent-up destructiveness to work "a kind of miracle" for the lost souls of this wild party: he triggers Irving Loon's psychosis by whispering to him the word "Windigo," the name of a terrible amoral Ojibwa deity.

The "miracle" that Siegel instigates is a purge of the decadent society towards which he has secretly harbored a great deal of fear. The Indian acts out Siegel's own paranoia and alienation. But the story is unconvincing because the catastrophe seems motivated more by the author's contrivance than by character development. It introduces several typical Pynchonian motifs, however, such as the paranoiac repression inflicted on minority races by white civilization, the satire of "hip" decadence, and the tenuous thread restraining apocalyptic violence in our society.

In Pynchon's next story, "Low-lands" (1960), the theme of the average man's confrontation with the wasteland of modern life is further developed. Dennis Flange and his wife live in a "curious, moss-thatched, almost organic mound" on Long Island Sound, which he calls his "womb with a view." After a gestation period of seven years of marriage, Flange is ejected. His wife tires of his habit of roistering with the garbage man, and when Pig Bodine, Flange's particularly scurrilous sailor friend, shows up, she throws out the lot. Retreating rather gladly from his wife's "relentless rationality" (Mondriaan is her favorite painter), Flange ends up that night in the dead center of the low country, the city dump. Lowlands represent to him a refuge from the possibility of "convexity," of being left sticking out, exposed to uncontrollable change, alone and unprotected.

Sleeping in the shack of Bolingbroke, proprietor of the dump, Flange is awakened by the dreamy voice of a woman. Entranced, he investigates and discovers a gypsy named Nerissa, only three and a half feet tall. She takes him to lands lower still: down through a network of tunnels in the mass of debris. They finally reach a little room at the bottom where she lives. He looks in her eyes and sees the sea, "the true mother image of us all": "whitecaps danced across her eyes; sea creatures, he knew, would be cruising about in the submarine green of her heart." Flange decides to stay with her. He strongly resembles Prufrock in T. S. Eliot's poem "The Love Song of J. Alfred Prufrock," who falls under the spell of the mermaids of his dreams:

> "We have lingered in the chambers of the sea
> By sea-girls wreathed with seaweed red and brown
> Till human voices wake us, and we drown."

No voices wake Flange, however: he has attained the lowest of lands and and the ultimate passivity. The sea is a wasteland to him; nevertheless, he embraces it because it recalls days as a sailor when he was in his prime, "Fortune's elf child." The tiny gypsy girl is clearly a female doppelganger image of his former idealized self, and a catalyst for his regression to a past state. His new womb has no view at all; it is a "dead end," a room inside the very earth. The gypsy's rat Hyacinth will substitute for the child he and his wife never had.

Cleanth Siegel responded to his wasteland with Kurtz's paranoiac philosophy: "Exterminate all the brutes." Dennis Flange chooses to withdraw further into the wasteland, to extinguish all possibility of action, of vulnerability. Violence and escapism are two kindred responses to alienation that are typical of Pynchon's later characters. Both indicate a disintegration of consciousness, an increasing disorderliness in the modern psyche. Neither course allows the fragmented ego to come back into touch with others, with the world, or with the deeper levels of the self.

In "Entropy" (1960), Pynchon achieves his most complete and effective exposition of this theme in the short stories. Entropy is the measure of randomness or disorder in a physical system. The Second Law of Thermodynamics states that entropy tends to increase when hot and cold molecules interact, until heat is uniformly distributed and no further activity is possible. Thus, greater disorder is associated with greater homogeneity. In this story Pynchon uses the value-neutral scientific term of entropy as a metaphor to connect decadence and erosion of moral values with mindless, passive conformity. The social and moral judgments become that much more powerful.

In Meatball Mulligan's apartment, a party has been going on for nearly two days. The guests are a mixed bag of pot-smoking jazz musicians, girls who work for the government, pseudo-intellectuals, and drunken sailors. They prefigure those marathon revelers of *V.*, the Whole Sick Crew. The party is noisy, and noise in the form of aimless, redundant language permeates the conversation. Entropy is evident in the breakdown of communication. The jazz group tries to circumvent the noise problem by playing a tune without their instruments, purely by thinking the music, but even in silence they cannot seem to stay in the same key. This futile exercise typifies the Absurdist approach to trying to escape environmental entropy: denying the very possibility of communication and meaning.

Above Meatball's apartment lives Callisto, a man obsessed with eradicating entropy from his life. To that end he has built for his girlfriend Aubade and himself a "hothouse jungle," an orderly little world filled with plant life, birds, and, of course, themselves as Adam and Eve to make the paradise complete: "Hermetically sealed, it was a tiny enclave of regularity in the city's chaos, alien to the vagaries of the weather, of national politics, of any civil disorder." Callisto has attempted to isolate himself from the outside world which, according to the cosmologists, is drifting towards an apocalyptic heat-death, a condition of total entropy. Callisto feels that extinction is around the corner, and the strange behavior of his outside thermometer tends to confirm his suspicions. Despite the varied weather of the past few days—rain, snow, sun, and gales—the temperature has remained steady at 37 degrees. This stasis causes him to fear the imminence of a state of perfect homogeneity, when the world has run down and no further motion is possible.

It takes a great deal of energy for him and Aubade to maintain their mental equilibrium in this paranoid enclave. The girl's fragile balance of awareness of artistic harmony over noise is threatened by such "hints of anarchy" from the apartment below as the thuddings and honkings of jazz records. She strains to maintain her balance while Callisto obliviously dictates his memoirs, envisioning a heat-death for the entropic culture outside and an indefinite perpetuation of his hothouse retreat.

What he forgets is that entropy tends to increase in any closed system— such as his apartment. The disorder in his environment can be calculated in terms of his and Aubade's narcissistic, self-centered lives. Having repressed their human need for change and growth, they glimpse chaos outside the closed rooms of their conscious minds. Just as it is impossible for anyone to *try* not to think, Aubade finds it impossible to concentrate on shutting out the entropic noise in her head; the irritating jazz music from Meatball's apartment is only a symptom of the unease, not the cause. In desperation she smashes the window with her bare hands: "and turned to face the man on the bed and wait with him until the moment of equilibrium was reached, when 37 degrees Fahrenheit should prevail both outside and inside, and forever, and the hovering, curious dominant of their separate lives should resolve into a tonic of darkness and the final absence of all motion." The Second Law of Thermodynamics has caught up with Callisto at last.

Meatball, on the other hand, finds a way to counteract the increasing disorderliness of his environment. Confronted with the choice of retreating into a closet until everybody goes away or trying to do something about the noise and chaos, Meatball eschews Callisto's path of withdrawal and decides to act. He manages to calm his guests down, one by one, restoring order to the environment through application of intelligence.

Human energy and intelligence are the regenerative potential in an otherwise decaying closed system, but Callisto paranoiacally isolates his intelligence from the outside world and thus makes himself even more susceptible to entropy. Entropic factors must be actively counteracted; they cannot be merely ignored. Human freedom is the variable factor in the thermodynamic equation: one can choose to acquiesce to the entropy, becoming part of the chaos, like Meatball's friends; one can try to shut it out, as Callisto does unsuccessfully; or one can attempt to rearrange a disintegrating environment so that it better resembles the coherent thought processes of one's own mind, as Meatball does successfully.

As a character observed in "Low-lands," there is a scientific principle that even an act of simple observation changes the thing being observed. This is a reference to the Heisenberg Uncertainty Principle, which holds that it is impossible to measure precisely the speed and position of subatomic particles. The very act of observation disturbs them. The whole notion of cause and effect, which is based on the assumption that a thing can be measured, is invalid on the subatomic level. By extension, though we can talk of cause and effect on the level of the large objects we can measure, the uncertainty principle limits the absoluteness of the principle of causality and affirms the inseparability of the subject and object of perception. In "Entropy" Pynchon implies that no one can exist in an environment without interacting with it and affecting its course towards greater or less entropy.

A conspiracy against entropy is the theme of "The Secret Integration" (1964). In the town of Mingebourough, Massachusetts, a boy genius named Grover and his friends form the first Pynchon "counterforce" (which we will see again in *The Crying of Lot 49* and *Gravity's Rainbow*): they organize against their parents and the whole adult society. They marshal other children to fight an annual mock-battle called Operation Spartacus after the movie about the Roman slave revolt; they ransack abandoned houses for antique furniture to sell; they infiltrate the PTA; they funnel sympathizers' milk money into their own fund; they sabotage the local paper mill, stop trains, explode sodium bombs, and let air out of tires. These are more than pranks: they are means of allowing a little reality to filter through the bars of small town conventionality into the children's lives.

When the Barringtons, a black couple, move into the white neighborhood, the children's parents make harassing phone calls and even dump their garbage on the Barringtons' lawn. In a "secret integration" of their own, the kids admit an imaginary black child, Carl Barrington, into their inner circle. But eventually they have to abandon their conspiracies, their Operation Spartacus, and even Carl; despite the injustice of their parents' prejudice, they depend on them too much for their security to carry the revolt any further. The revelation of the extent of the evil in their parents disillusions them, crushes them for the present. They return to their homes, to "hot shower, dry towel, good night kiss, and dreams that could never again be entirely safe." Dreams have been the means through which reality was integrated into their lives. Growing up, they must come to grips with the adult world and make a new integration, while not forgetting that unconventional dream-vision of reality.

Counterforces, as paranoid subcultures, are subject to entropy. They cannot reduce the entropy in the outside world unless they interact positively with the world. The children of "The Secret Integration" are simply in revolt; they cannot communicate their more humane, unprejudiced vision to their parents, and they cannot even clearly articulate their attitudes to themselves. They react instinctively, but their effort is doomed because as children they are too dependent—psychologically as well as materially— upon their parents to take the step toward effective challenge. Pynchon leaves us at the end with no assurances that the children will successfully renew the entropic world once they mature, but the temporary framework of their counterforce is a step in that direction.

In addition to these four stories, Pynchon wrote an article about black subculture, "A Journey Into the Mind of Watts" (1966), in the wake of Los Angeles's 1965 Watts riots. To him, Watts is "a pocket of bitter reality" in contrast with the safe, shallow, media-manufactured, escapist dream that Southern Californian white society lives in. This is a powerful piece of journalism, full of sympathy for those blacks for whom violence and defeat are a way of life. Blacks are menaced by gun-toting white cops, harassed by social workers into homogenizing themselves to fit white society's standards, and consistently thwarted in their attempts to improve their condition.

The article is less social description, however, than a commentary on two different states of mind. One, the white, is captured in an image of secretaries chatting the afternoon away, complaining about malfunctioning computers, while "inspirational mottoes like SMILE decorate the beaverboard office walls along with. . .clippings from the slick magazines about 'What Is Emotional Maturity?' " Whatever it is, it must surely include a dose of Watts-style reality, the other state of mind. This state Pynchon captures in his final image of an art object made from a hollow TV set smashed in the riots: "inside, where its picture tube should have been, gazing out with scorched wiring threaded like electronic ivy among its crevices and sockets, was a human skull. The name of the piece was 'The Late, Late, Late Show.' " Both sensibilities are paranoid: the whites fear the "terrible vitality" Watts represents, a violent power for upheaval; the blacks fear the whites but are more realistic about what they are up against. They see the face of white media-land entropy—the skull in the television.

From the polarization of the two opposite, paranoid states of mind grew the entropic forces that fueled the Watts riots. Each state of mind is a closed system, and Pynchon's prescription is clear: the minds must be opened. Creativity and intelligence must be channeled into integrating the cultures, dissipating hostilities, awakening to the realities of different modes of perception—or society as a whole will fail. But the differences must be respected, not homogenized out as the whites would like; for the measure of disorder only increases when the uniqueness of the individual point of view is absorbed by the mass mind. Life proceeds on the basis of a harmoniously functioning organization of individual cells.

The problem of a society in deterioration pervades all of Pynchon's short work, and he has already begun to suggest through literary and scientific allusions the universal scope of man's fight against entropy. He has analyzed the paranoid response in its destructive and creative forms; delved into the special relationship of minorities to the dominant society; suggested the apocalyptic consequences of blind cooperation with the tides of entropy sweeping through our lives. Artistically the stories are interesting, but especially so in light of the novels that follow them. In *V.* Pynchon goes far beyond these early formulations and invests the entropy problem with the dimensions of history, myth, religion, and philosophy.

Chapter Two
CHERCHEZ LA FEMME

Pynchon's first novel is a mystery for the reader to solve. One of the characters, Herbert Stencil, is searching for clues to substantiate the identity of a mysterious woman he calls V., who had apparently been involved in fomenting crises in the Western world throughout the century. We follow his quest, gradually picking up the implied associations between episodes where V. appears, and try to decide to what extent Stencil is manufacturing those correspondences. We must also relate Stencil's quest through the past to the adventures of his acquaintances in the present.

The "present," actually, is New York in 1956, but it is not so far removed from our own time that Pynchon's satire is irrelevant. The episodes in this time period are full of the doings of Benny Profane and his friends, known as "the Whole Sick Crew," and several individuals tangential to the group. Profane is a "schlemihl" and a "yo-yo," a fat, horny, pig-eyed ex-Navy man who drifts from place to place, job to job, woman to woman, without much apparent self-awareness or purpose in life. He inhabits the Street—that zone of perpetual transition, an eternal Now and Nowhere—yet he is not at home in it. Inanimate objects tyrannize him; he has no adeptness at gaining control of his environment: "Streets. . .had taught him nothing: he couldn't work a transit, crane, payloader, couldn't lay bricks, stretch a tape right, hold an elevation rod still, hadn't even learned to drive a car. He walked; walked, he thought sometimes, the aisles of a bright, gigantic supermarket, his only function to want" (p.27). It is somewhat difficult to explain Profane's sexual attractiveness, as he seems to give little to the women he is involved with. He only takes. He avoids dependents and responsibilities. Yet this curious, neutral character has one outstanding trait: he is outrageously funny. Whatever bizarre happenstance befalls him, his response is a simple, declarative "Wha." Not "Wha?"—that would show too much commitment. It is the monosyllable of disorientation, the helpless, awestruck reflex of a passive Everyman to the incursions of an alien, inanimate Other.

Profane's women include Rachel Owlglass, who likes to mother him (she controls an invisible umbilical yo-yo string attached to his navel); Paola Maijstral Hod, a taciturn, enigmatic Maltese beauty who occasionally looks to him for protection from the advances of the satyr Pig Bodine; and Fina Mendoza, a Puerto Rican virgin who tries unsuccessfully to seduce the indifferent Profane. Profane forms no lasting attachments; he yo-yos back and forth among the women. The three embody different archetypal feminine aspects: the maternal though tiny Rachel aids Profane from her position at the Space/Time Employment Agency and helps finance her roommate Esther's abortion and nose job; Fina is the holy virgin, a spiritual leader of a youth gang called the Playboys—who eventually commit sacrilege and gangbang her; Paola is the image of mysterious beauty, and the inheritor of the positive aspects of V.'s mythic role, as we shall see later.

The members of the Whole Sick Crew represent variations on modern decadence. They spend most of their time drinking, partying, and conversing in proper nouns; they are pseudo-intellectual name droppers: "It was the unhappy fact that most of them worked for a living and obtained the substance of their conversation from the pages of *Time* magazine and like publications" (p.46). Like the roisterers in Meatball Mulligan's apartment in "Entropy," the Crew are entropic. They imitate the forms of artistic expression rather than display true creativity. For instance, the painter Slab is a "Catatonic Expressionist" who turns out canvas after canvas of cheese Danishes in various surrealistic contexts. Mafia Winsome is a popular writer of long novels which glorify Heroic Love between "godlike, inexhaustible sexual athletes," "tall, strong, white though often robustly tanned (all over), Anglo-Saxon, Teutonic, and/or Scandinavian" (p.113). Her husband Roony is a record company executive who lusts after Paola while letting the Crew—

who sleep on his floor—cavort with the nymphomaniac Mafia. And Pig Bodine, perhaps the funniest character in Pynchon's novels, is a Neanderthal in sailor's uniform, a hairy, gross guzzler of grog with an obscene laugh ("Hyeugh, hyeugh") who nevertheless can talk Sartre when he's in the mood.

Behind the satire and the farce of bohemian decadence is a darker vision of a twentieth century wasteland. The Crew are in danger of losing their humanity, becoming inanimate objects. In their conversations they play with permutations of proper nouns, rearranging them inside a closed system of finite possibilities. The closed system is entropic: "This sort of arranging and rearranging was Decadence, but the exhaustion of all possible permutations and combinations was death" (p.277). One very far-gone Crew member, Fergus Mixolydian, is a mere electronic extension of his TV set. When he is awake, electrodes in his skin trigger the set's switch automatically, and he never has to get out of bed. His life system is closed, and creativity has been channeled into inventing a way to dull waking consciousness, to return life to an inanimate state.

Benny Profane's awkwardness with inanimate objects is due to the fact that he is something of an inanimate lump of flesh himself. In a dream he unscrews a bolt in his navel and his ass falls off; walking down the Street of his dreams, he wonders if the rest of his body will fall apart: "If he kept going down that street, not only his ass but also his arms, legs, sponge brain and clock of a heart must be left behind to litter the pavement, be scattered among manhole covers" (p.30). Profane's great fear is that he is a machine without a soul, like the simulacra SHROUD and SHOCK who are systematically destroyed in "accident research" at Anthroresearch Associates, where he works for a time. SHROUD, with its grinning skull-face, "talks" to Profane, mocking as illusion the notion that he and the rest of the human race are animate creatures. SHOCK, like a schlemihl, gets smashed up in test automobiles; SHROUD predicts everybody will become like it and SHOCK someday—totally inanimate, and at the mercy of destructive external forces.

Esther Harvitz is afflicted by a similar passivity. She submits to a nose job from Dr. Schoenmaker which is described in graphically sexual terms, and later has a sexual relationship with the doctor, who seeks to remake her physically to correspond to his ideal image. During the operation her desire for oblivion is realized: "It was almost a mystic experience. What religion is it—one of the Eastern ones—where the highest condition we can attain is that of an object—a rock. It was like that; I felt myself drifting down, this delicious loss of Estherhood, becoming more and more a blob, with no worries, traumas, nothing: only Being..." (p.93).

In this parody of genuine transcendental experience, Pynchon exposes the facile analogies with which many are willing to rationalize their descent to inanimateness and their sacrifice of freedom of choice. Esther puts herself in service to the abstract idea of ideal beauty, and thinks by that means to lose the burden of her individual humanness.

To his credit Profane does not try to rationalize his schlemihlhood. As he does not believe he has control of his own life, he cannot take effective action to reverse its entropy. He sees clearly that the whole world is in a process of disintegration. For a time he ventures beneath the Street: in the sewers he hunts alligators—a lowly job, as low as he can go—but it is his way of attempting to get underneath the superficiality of ordinary society, the "people in new suits, millions of inanimate objects being produced brand-new every week, new cars in the streets, houses going up by the thousands all over the suburbs he had left months ago" (p.134). Like Dennis Flange in "Lowlands," he is a dropout from the pursuit of the shining ideal of the New which everyone else worships. The New is perpetually deteriorating because it is designed for obsolescence. Profane has a nostalgia for the Depression and identifies with "every no-name drifter, mooch, square's tenant" (p.335). That is why he pities the alligators he must shoot. They have been adopted by kids as pets, then flushed down toilets; like them, Profane finds in the sewers a temporary haven. As in *Gravity's Rainbow*, where the passage down the toilet will represent a period of withdrawal and communal renewal for the dispossessed of the earth, so here Profane is renewed through his identification with his kindred spirits, the alligators: "Almost as if there had been this agreement, a covenant, Profane giving death, the alligators giving him employment: tit for tat." They are "falsely animated kids' toys" (p.133), like "yo-yo" Profane. When he feels the umbilical tug of Rachel's yo-yo string, Profane must return to Street level.

Rachel is one of the most sympathetic characters in the book; she tries to shake Profane out of his lethargy, gets him jobs, tries to get him to care about her. His affections are transitory because he *is* profane: the nature of non-sacred reality is ever-changing, and Profane is incapable of being anchored in universal truths or feelings—such as love. But Rachel is contradictory: she too partakes of inanimateness. When he first met her she had an MG sports car which she liked to fondle while breathing such phrases as "You beautiful stud" (p.19). In Profane's eyes, she is an accessory to the car, as she is clearly only an accessory to his life, a little mother-figure who keeps him in her womb, as it were. Their union is like the covenant between Profane and the alligators: "Screwer and screwee. On this foundation, perhaps, the island stood, from the bottom of the lowest sewer bed to the tip of the TV antenna on top of the Empire Building" (p.40).

Profane occasionally indulges in one of the Crew's favorite pastimes, yo-yoing on the subway. This simply means riding on the same line, back and forth, for as long as possible. The meaningless repetition of experience, sought for its own sake, is a sign of entropy, of the decrease of energy and life in a closed system. All Profane's wanderings in his Street reduce to one line that means nothing.

At the end of the novel, in Valletta, Malta, Profane has broken up at last with Paola. She has gone back to her husband, and Profane is left feeling like a "schlemihl redeemer" standing, rather than walking, on the sea— "while that enormous malingering city and its one livable inner space and one unconnable (therefore hi-valu) girl had all slid away from him over a great horizon's curve. . ." (p.427). He takes up with Brenda Wigglesworth, an American college girl who is fascinated with him because of all his "fabulous experiences," but Profane demurs, "offhand I'd say I haven't learned a goddamn thing." He has known the decadence she is trying to experience—and attempts to express through a sophomoric poem ("I am the twentieth century. . .I am the virgin's-hair whip and the cunningly detailed shackles of decadent passion. . .". Her images encapsulate most of the main themes of the novel, but she doesn't understand their significance; they are ideas she has picked up in her classes. Profane, on the other hand, is depressed because he has experienced the lengths of the street and the depths of the sewers and is no wiser or happier for it. His fate is ambiguous: he and Brenda disappear into the "abruptly absolute night" (p.428) as they run down a street—the same Street Profane has been yo-yoing on throughout the novel.

In the Street of the twentieth century, sex is reduced to a mechanical activity. Not only do many characters, such as Mafia, copulate with a machine-like resolution, but actual mechanical appurtenances begin to usurp sexual functions. There is Rachel's erotic MG and Schoenmaker's nasal "rape" of Esther with surgical instruments; there is the camera of Morris Teflon, used voyeuristically on unsuspecting couples sleeping in his apartment; there is the .30-caliber machine gun of Da Conho, the Brazilian Zionist, who fantasizes killing Arabs while Yemenite girls' loins ache with love for him. The maternal function also succumbs to entropy in the opening scene of the novel. In the Sailor's Grave, a bar run by Beatrice Buffo, all the barmaids are known as Beatrice on the theory that "just as small children call all females mother, so sailors, in their way equally as helpless, should call all barmaids Beatrice" (p.4). The Sailor's Grave offers further mothering during Suck Hour, a periodic celebration in which dozens of sailors guzzle gallons of free brew from foam beer taps shaped like large breasts.

Sexual energy, creative energy, the moral energy to choose alternatives: these are exhausted in the twentieth century wasteland. But Pynchon's satire of the present scene is not scathing. Profane and the Whole Sick Crew are to be taken as lightly as the buffoonery and low comedy in Shakespeare's plays. They constitute, in fact, a healthy contrast with the episodes about V., in which decadence has a much less comic significance.

The information about V. is fragmentary, and we have to put it together ourselves, like pieces of a puzzle, following the lead of the monomaniac Herbert Stencil, but taking into account the fact that much of the information has been "Stencilized"—processed through the filter of his mind. Stencil's obsession to prove V.'s existence and establish her historical significance is a tendency counter to Profane's passive acceptance of the entropic world. Like Callisto in "Entropy," Stencil creates a hothouse, a controlled environment—albeit an intellectual one—in which some order can be maintained. V. is his organizing principle for understanding the chaos of modern life. She is, in fact, the mother of chaos, as he sees it.

We yo-yo between episodes of the Street (the present-day world of Profane and the Crew) and the hothouse of the past (scenes of V.'s life). She first appears in Cairo in 1898 as Victoria Wren, innocent, 18-year-old daughter of an English peer who is the target of anarchist plots. From the random observations of outsiders we piece together the story: a spy named Goodfellow seduces her; he is opposed by another spy, Bongo-Shaftesbury, who, during a skirmish involving the girl, kills Porpentine, Goodfellow's friend. The backdrop of this episode is a political crisis between Britain and France known as the Fashoda Incident. These colonialist powers, struggling for territorial rights in Africa, represent an exploitative attitude that surfaces among the tourists as the Baedeker view of life—that is, the substitution of the superficial, guidebook aspect of a foreign land for the beneath-the-skin reality.

Victoria is living in Baedekerland at the outset. She has flirted with the Catholic Church and the prospect of becoming a sister, "had indeed for a time considered the Son of God as a young lady will consider any eligible bachelor." But unwilling to compete with the "great harem clad in black" for His attention, she turns to mortal men. Yet Victoria (the namesake of the matron of the British Empire) has power fantasies that mingle with her sexual and religious yearnings; her world is that of a colonial doll that "she could play with and within constantly: developing, exploring, manipulating" (p.61). As the embodiment of the naive colonialist and tourist attitude towards the foreign, fascinated by it as by a dark mystery whose heart can be plucked out and held up to the light of rationality, she shows potentialities for corruption even in her innocence.

The following year she reappears in Florence amidst a suspected plot involving an obscure country called Vheissu, a kind of Shangri-la discovered by the explorer, Captain Hugh Godolphin. It is no ideal civilization: "There's barbarity, insurrection, internecine feud." But its colors are magical: "The trees outside the head shaman's house have spider monkeys which are iridescent. They change color in the sunlight. . . . No sequence of colors is the same from day to day. As if you lived inside a madman's kaleidoscope. Even your dreams become flooded with colors, with shapes no Occidental ever saw. Not real shapes, not meaningful ones. Simply random. . ." (p.155). It is widely suspected that there is imminent, apocalyptic danger connected with this land; one version of the plot is that this barbaric race is preparing to invade or infiltrate the rest of the world through a secret network of subterranean tunnels. The British mind cannot hold these wonders; it responds in sadistic terror to these glimpses of mystery, as to "a dark woman tattooed from head to toe" (p.156) whom it feels compelled to flay. The coded, incomprehensible surface of the Other is fearsome to the colonialist's psyche; he fears that there is nothing underneath it and is driven to expose that nothingness in order to confirm his own tenuous existence.

The Baedekerland tourist contents himself with the "skin" of the foreign country because he cannot bear change. He projects surface complexity and internal hollowness upon the Other because that is what he sees inside himself. His desire to see the world is a quasi-erotic one, to have "caressed the skin of each alien place" (p.168), and is akin to the power fantasies of the colonialist who must flay that "glittering integument" (p.169) from the barbarous body of the exotic Other.

It is never clear whether fears of Vheissu are mere paranoia. But there are other plots afoot in Florence: an uprising among the Venezuelans in the city, and an attempt to steal Botticelli's *Birth of Venus* from the Uffizi. The recurrence of the letter V in these matters gives added significance to the presence of Victoria Wren, who has by now become a "self-proclaimed. . . citizen of the world" (p.151), severing ties with her family and with England. She is becoming a country unto herself, and her religion is also self-centered: she has already had four love affairs which she sees "as outward and visible signs of an inward spiritual grace belonging to Victoria alone" (p.152). Sex is a substitute for her unfulfilled cravings for Christ, and as such has spiritual power. Victoria has little direct connection with the chaos around her, but she seems to embody the disintegrative forces at work. In herself she is still innocent, a feminine ideal, like the rioting Venezuelans' personification of Liberty, or Botticelli's Venus, the object of Signor Mantissa's larcenous lust. But she has an evil influence: this at least is Stencil's conclusion. She joins in the violence of the riot at last, flaying the face of a policeman with her fingernails.

V. next appears in Paris in 1913 as a wealthy lady in love with a fifteen-year-old dancer named Melanie l'Heuremaudit. V. has adopted the period trappings of decadence: African and Oriental decor, black cigarettes, and "a circle inclined toward sadism, sacrilege, endogamy, and homosexuality" (p.382). Melanie, her fetish, gives her sexual pleasure by watching her in a mirror; the girl becomes her very "double" in a peculiarly mental kind of love play. V. is able to be her own voyeur by identifying with the watching Melanie. Melanie and V. are reduced to inanimate statues, a kind of death echoing the medieval theme that "the act of love and the act of death are one." Decadence, identified throughout the novel with the entropic tendency toward inanimateness, is now almost complete: "Dead at last, they would be one with the inanimate universe and with each other" (p.385). Melanie in fact is literally sacrificed during a ballet performance: playing a virgin to be impaled on a pole, she forgets to wear her protective device and dies gruesomely on stage. The fault, it is implied, is partly V.'s: "Adorned with so many combs, bracelets, sequins, [Melanie] might have become confused in this fetish-world and neglected to add to herself the one inanimate object that would have saved her" (p.389). The performance itself "has been connected along with Russia to an international movement seeking to over-throw Western civilization" (p.387), and a riot ensues reminiscent of the premiere of Stravinsky's *Rite of Spring*. V.'s presence is again connected with social turmoil and death.

She reappears in 1919 on Malta during a time of more political distur-bances, revolutionary activity against the colonialist British. Sidney Stencil, father of Herbert, is engaged there in intelligence work for the British Foreign Office. He had been a lover of Victoria Wren in Florence in 1899, and he encounters her again here as Veronica Manganese, her name sug-gestive of her "obsession with bodily incorporating little bits of inert matter" (p.459). They resume their intimacies. She has a false eye in the form of a clock, signifying the disintegrative drift of time, and a star sapphire sewn into her navel; she desires an artificial foot as well, which she later gets. Evan Godolphin, son of Hugh, is her caretaker; he is hideously disfigured due to the failure of plastic surgery following a World War I injury. Ironi-cally, it was the injection of inanimate substances into his facial tissue that produced the disaster—and inspired young Schoenmaker, who had worshipped Godolphin, to dedicate his life to plastic surgery. Thus the past casts its nets into the present, especially with reference to the encroachment of the inanimate upon life.

V. still appears to have some feeling for the Church; she goes to mass and confession. Yet she enjoys gazing upon Nothingness with her dead clock-eye, and she arranges for the Banditti to kill Dupiro, an informer for the British who is in love with one of her maids. Her own political sympathies are uncertain; she seems to encourage all dissident elements. But her implied influence in this episode goes beyond her actions. Old Stencil associates her with the apocalyptic drift of the time: "The matter of a Paraclete's coming, the comforter, the dove; the tongues of flame, the gift of tongues: Pentecost. Third Person of the Trinity. None of it was implausible to Stencil. The Father had come and gone. In political terms, the Father was the Prince; the single leader, the dynamic figure whose *virtu* used to be a determinant of history. This had degenerated to the Son, genius of the liberal love-feast which had produced 1848 and lately the overthrow of the Czars. What next? What Apocalypse? Especially on Malta, a matriarchal island. Would the Paraclete be also a mother?" (p.444). *Virtu*, or human agency, has been eclipsed by the female goddess Fortuna, associated here with the Paraclete or Holy Spirit. The feminine power arises to challenge the masculine Father, who has been dominant throughout history with his *virtu*. In the destructive person of V., the Paraclete can only be bringing an end to civilization as we know it. Sidney Stencil's own life ends mysteriously at sea in a waterspout; the sinking ship's figurehead is Astarte, goddess of sexual love, and the associations with V. and the intertwining of the themes of sex and death suggest a supernatural connection between V. and the goddess.

In 1922 V. appears as Vera Meroving in South West Africa during an uprising of the Bondelzwarts against South African rule. An enclave of Germans barricade themselves in the estate house of a man called Foppl and carry on a marathon siege party for months. The guests titillate, torture, and abuse one another in a claustrophobic decadence reminiscent of Poe's "The Masque of the Red Death," in which a large party of corrupt rich are struck down by the plague they can shut out of their homes but not out of their hearts. Vera's lover is the transvestite Lieutenant Weissmann—later to be resurrected as Blicero in *Gravity's Rainbow*—who is the typically cold, paranoiac Nazi sadist. He decodes certain atmospheric radio transmissions called "sferics" received by Kurt Mondaugen, a young engineer, and derives the phrase "Die Welt ist alles was die Fall ist"—the world is all that is the case—from Ludwig Wittgenstein, a positivist philosopher. Wittgenstein denied the ability of language to encompass metaphysics, and defined the world as a closed system limited by experience and observation. It is appropriate that Weissmann should find in the sferics a philosophic statement that could be taken as his own commitment to a closed society in which favored individuals such as himself dominate and tyrannize the weak and powerless, such as the Bondels. This does not impugn Wittgenstein's philosophy as sadistic or entropic; William Plater has demonstrated the larger importance of the philosopher to Pynchon's work in *The Grim Phoenix: Reconstructing Thomas Pynchon*.

The decadence of the particular microcosm of Foppl's party is the most marked of any closed system in the novel. Even though Herbert Stencil associates the Whole Sick Crew with the degenerates of Foppl's, there is really no comparison. The Crew are mere amateurs in entropy; the Germans are professionals. This is the darkest chapter of V. and presages some equally painful passages in *Gravity's Rainbow*. Pynchon recalls German atrocities against the Hereros in 1904, when General Lothar von Trotha exterminated over 60,000 blacks in punishment for their recalcitrance. Von Trotha is Foppl's hero, and Foppl personally beats a number of Bondels to death with his sjambok, a heavy leather whip. Pynchon does not shrink from portraying the ultimate consequences of the entropic slide towards inanimateness.

Vera has an adolescent alter ego in this episode reminiscent of Melanie l'Heuremaudit. Her name is Hedwig Vogelsang, and her "purpose on earth is to tantalize and send raving the race of man" (p.221). She is coquettish with Mondaugen until he falls deathly ill with scurvy, at which point she makes love to him indefatigably, while Vera satisfies herself perversely with the aged Hugh Godolphin, who is also ill. The two V.'s have consecrated their sexuality to the love of death and seem to infect all around them with the same obsession.

V.'s final appearance is in Valletta, Malta, during World War II in an episode narrated by Fausto Maijstral, father of Paola. The island is being heavily bombed by Italian and German planes, and there is also an assault on its religious values in the person of the Bad Priest—V. in disguise. She tries to coerce the children into anti-life attitudes: the girls to "avoid the sensual extremes—pleasure of intercourse, pain of childbirth," the boys to be "like a crystal: beautiful and soulless" (p.319). She urges them to become identified with the rocky immortality of the island of Malta, to become, like her, inanimate. Fausto himself goes through several transformations: at first he wants to be a priest, as Victoria Wren had originally desired to be a nun; then he moves into a state of inanimateness, "the lowest form of consciousness" (p.294), a retreat from the pain of the bombings. The critical event that enables him to move from this living death back into a new life, with a consciousness that can reflect upon, accept, and express his past is the death of V.

As the Bad Priest, she is injured in a raid, trapped under a fallen beam in a ruined house. As Fausto watches, the children, whose "view of death was non-human" (p.311), disassemble V., ignoring her entreaties for help, removing her glass eye, her false teeth, her artificial foot, her navel sapphire. Fausto envisons her whole body as inanimate: "Surely her arms and breasts could be detached; the skin of her legs peeled away to reveal some intricate understructure of silver openwork. Perhaps the trunk itself contained other wonders: intestines of parti-coloured silk, gay balloon-lungs, a rococo heart." In her dying cries, however, he detects "a sincere hatred for all her sins which must have been countless; a profound sorrow at having hurt God by sinning; a fear of losing Him which was worse than the fear of death" (p.322). The fact that V. seems to perform a perfect act of contrition is very important in our assessment of her ultimate significance. She cannot be seen totally as a destructive force, the embodiment of entropy, if she makes peace with the spirit of creativity.

To Herbert Stencil, V. is the possible ordering principle in the chaos of world events, the explanation for the disintegrative tendencies in modern life. But V. is not just the individual who was born Victoria Wren in 1880 and died the Bad Priest in 1943. She is also Venus, Vheissu, Queen Victoria, the Holy Virgin, Valletta, Venezuela, Vesuvius, a sewer rat named Veronica, a woman's spread thighs, formations of migrating birds. In short, V. may be found everywhere. Stencil "stencilizes" all his perceptions with the letter V, seeking a higher order in the world beyond what is apparent to the senses, even to the point of abstracting himself out of the world: he never refers to himself other than in the third person. In this respect he is compared to Henry Adams, who used the same technique in his autobiography *The Education of Henry Adams* (1918). Adams conceived the Virgin as the motive force throughout Western history, and noted that the Dynamo was replacing her as the paradigm for power in modern life. Science was usurping the supremacy of religion, and the religious frame of reference, in which God is an absolute, was being replaced by the relativistic frame in which all knowledge of reality is conditioned by the observer's point of view. Stencil unites both the Virgin and the Dynamo in V., an image of divine female power that is mechanized, a force that draws the world, including herself, into entropic decline.

Through the very act of observation, and despite his attempts at objectivity, Stencil colors his perceptions. He is the classic Pynchon paranoid who structures his universe around the idea of a Cosmic Plot. Stencil can never be sure of the real significance of the bits of historical information he culls; he cannot tell to what extent the V. pattern is the one he discovers or the one he projects. Furthermore, he is chary of finding out too much by going to Malta, where his father had died. What psychologists would call an "approach-avoidance syndrome" keeps him actively questing for V. but never discovering the final secret. He shies away from completing the search.

He almost does overcome his fear of reaching the goal of his quest. At the end of the novel he, Paola, and Profane travel to Malta where it is possible to follow the leads from Fausto's story. But he leaves prematurely, following the trail of "one Mme. Viola, oneiromancer and hypnotist, who passed through Valletta in 1944" (p.425). She is supposed to have V.'s glass eye in her possession. An oneiromancer is a diviner through dreams, and Stencil's particular waking dream is not to be dissolved through yet another manifestation of V., the dream weaver.

If Stencil had paid more attention to the here and now, he might have noticed that Paola wore a comb depicting five crucified British soldiers. This was V.'s comb, bought in Cairo in 1898, and stolen from her body by one of the Maltese children—presumably Paola herself. Thus she becomes V.'s principal beneficiary and possibly a new manifestation of what V. represents.

Paola has none of the decadent leanings of V., however. She is rather aloof from the Crew, absolutely repulsed by Pig Bodine, and even goes underground for a while, adopting an alternate frame of reference to open her life to new meaning. She impersonates a black prostitute and becomes the lover of McClintock Sphere, a jazz musician. Sphere's motto is "keep cool, but care" (p.342-343), a principle which Paola learns to incorporate in her life. In Malta she meets with Pappy Hod, her estranged husband, and promises to wait faithfully for his return to the States, like Penelope for Odysseus. To seal the compact she hands him V.'s comb. She can now care for Pappy without losing her cool; her equanimity will no longer be shaken by his erratic behavior.

The comb, with its symbolism of sacrifice, is as appropriate to Paola's self-sacrificing attitude as it is to V.'s own crucifying dismemberment. Pynchon evokes both positive and negative poles of meaning through the image: sacrificial death is a ritual dying into life. Indeed, V.'s repentance as she dies indicates transcendence of the closed system in which she has been deteriorating for so many years, and Paola's acceptance of Pappy shows a transformation has occurred that has totally altered the coordinates of her old life.

There are two V.s, really—the historical and the archetypal. The historical V. clearly has little direct causal connection to the chaotic events that surround her, and her relationship to "The Big One, the century's master cabal," though imagined by Stencil, is never demonstrated. But Stencil's conception of V. goes beyond the woman born Victoria Wren: "If she were a historical fact then she continued active today and at the moment, because the ultimate Plot Which Has No Name was as yet unrealized, though V. might be no more a she than a sailing vessel or a nation" (p.210). If V. is, in fact, the sailing vessel with the figurehead of Astarte on which Sidney Stencil meets his death, or the nation Vheissu, if she can paradoxically be seen as an asexual creature, as is sometimes hinted, then V. is no longer a historical individual but an archetype.

An archetype is a primordial image which recurs in art, myth, literature, and dreams in different cultures at different times. Pynchon himself mentions Stencil's quest in relation to Robert Graves's book *The White Goddess*, a study of the archetypal female figure. Erich Neumann, another mythographer, has schematized in *The Great Mother* the different manifestations of the Mother Goddess in a manner very helpful to our understanding of V. The Great Mother has a creative aspect symbolized by her receptive womb. The association of the maternal with the protective is very common, but there comes a time in everyone's psychic development when he must break away from the mother or he will never be able to stand on his own feet. A person with a weak ego or sense of self clings to the mother in a regressive longing for the security of the womb. At that moment the Good Mother changes into the Terrible Mother. The womb develops teeth. According to Neumann: "the destructive side of the Feminine, the destructive and deathly womb, appears most frequently in the archetypal form of a mouth bristling with teeth." The historical V. is a form of the Terrible Mother; her false teeth, which Stencil and Profane with great trouble steal from the dentist Eigenvalue, are made of different varieties of precious metals, suggesting the devouring maw of the earth, which—as the Cave—is an example of negative female vessel symbolism, according to Neumann. V.'s crucifying comb also suggests the *vagina dentata*.

Stencil has a weak ego; he cannot refer to himself in the first person and defines himself solely in terms of an unknown Other. He is "quite purely He Who Looks for V." (p.210); he impersonates an identity, as do all the members of the Crew. Thus the Terrible Mother consumes him. Though the pursuit of V. may destroy him, he will continue to search for her because he cannot seem to extricate himself from her teeth.

Neumann speaks of "the suction of the unconscious and its regressive lure" as constituting the terrible aspect of the Feminine. In Pynchon's terms, the gravity pulling man back into the cave of unconsciousness, into the womb of the inanimate, is entropy. And this pull is to be resisted if we are to survive. The wars, the refinement of destructive weapons, the slide into aesthetic, moral, and physical decadence are signs of the teeth of the Terrible Mother. Pynchon indicates possibilities for rebirth, as we have seen, but his implication is neither optimistic nor pessimistic. The past is a closed system whose energies have been steadily dissipating; the future is a field of all possibilities.

The island of Malta is "a cradle of life" (p.358) for these possibilities. "An immovable rock in the river Fortune" (p.305) during the war, it shares with its inhabitants rocklike qualities—tenacity, perseverance—a tendency towards the inanimate. Yet this kind of inanimateness enables them to endure. The personifications of Malta as a source of rocklike human strength, as an "inviolable womb" (p.298), as "Virgin assailed" and "winged mother protective" (p.317)—these metaphors enable the people of the island to survive as they imaginatively participate in the qualities of the Good Mother. But V., as the Bad Priest, is like "an evil spirit: alien, parasitic" (p.293), draining spiritual energy instead of nurturing it. The creative and destructive feminine aspects are at war. The Good Mother shelters the spark of consciousness in the rock of her womb, while the Terrible Mother tries to turn the hearts of men to stone. Yet both of these are V. in her archetypal character.

We can understand how they may coexist by recalling the image of the Paraclete, the Third Person of the Trinity. Insofar as V. is an incarnation of divine power, bringing down apocalypse on tongues of fire, she is scourger of the moribund, accelerating its total collapse. But she also serves the apocalyptic function of speaking the new Word of a new creation. Apocalypse is the end of history and a transfiguration of life into an utterly new form: profane becomes sacred; stencils become originals.

V. is associated at various times with Fortuna, the Roman goddess of Fate; with Mara and Astarte, goddesses of fertility; and Venus, goddess of love, as well as with the Virgin Mary. All of these ambiguous deities have both creative and destructive aspects. V. is not only a destructive entity: in Paola she is reborn as a spirit of potential regeneration for the modern wasteland. This possibility is only hinted at in *V.*, but Oedipa Maas will carry the theme a step further in *The Crying of Lot 49*.

Stencil's problem is that he takes the "plot" too literally. The historical V., together with her archetypal connections, is best seen as a metaphor for the sacred dimension of life. Paranoia for him is a secular religion that gives him a reason for living. But like so many conspiracy buffs, he becomes fascinated with the pattern he has created—until it becomes his primary reality. Pynchon does not denigrate paranoia; it is essential to survival for Slothrop in *Gravity's Rainbow*, and it can be useful as an alternative to the conventional notions of reality, to help one organize one's thoughts into new, more integrative patterns. It could be Stencil's pathway to the Mother Goddess, but he keeps V. on the secular level, getting sidetracked by the minutiae of her historical existence, the relics such as the teeth and the glass eye. She stays disintegrated.

V. represents the apocalyptic meaning of history, and Stencil avoids the future implications of that, preferring to stay in the hothouse of the past pursuing his clues. For him V. is merely destructive; she is an enigma which he must not solve if he is to continue touring the Baedekerland V.-womb rather than emerging and discovering the possibilities for redemptive change in the world outside the closed system of his mind.

Profane is Stencil's counterpart. He too goes nowhere, and is as fixed in his passivity as Stencil is in his obsession. Like all other comic characters they do not change: they keep making the same mistakes, slipping on the same banana peels. Representing two poles of comedy—that of the mono-maniac whose private vision controls his whole reality, and the anarchist clown who controls nothing and is buffeted by the winds of chance—Stencil and Profane form a pair analogous to Don Quixote and Sancho Panza.

V., on the other hand, is a tragic figure. She is aware of her self-destructive nature, even as it feeds on her innocence and corrupts those around her—but she cannot act to reverse the entropy. Her body becomes inanimate, becomes the wasteland, and no knight appears on the horizon to redeem her. Certainly Don Stencil does not quality. She lives and dies alone, yearning for oblivion but never managing to detach herself totally from her thirst for life. Her tragedy is that she never knows she is a goddess; she thinks she is an inanimate shell covering nothingness.

There is one character who transcends both the comedy and the tragedy. He is Mehemet, the wise old master of the ship that takes Sidney Stencil to Malta, and later, to his death. He sails with V. in the form of a figurehead of Astarte, a goddess he knows to be inconstant like Fortune. He under-stands entropy: "both the world and we, M. Stencil, began to die from the moment of birth" (p.432). Yet he does not try—as does the elder and later the younger Stencil—to rationalize the process: " 'Is old age a disease?' Mehemet asked. 'The body slows down, machines wear out, planets falter and loop, sun and stars gutter and smoke. Why say a disease? Only to bring it down to a size you can look at and feel comfortable?' " (p.433). Mehemet has had an experience of time-travel; his craft had once somehow slipped into the year 1324. Thus he knows that the boundaries of space and time are not absolute; they are a function of our point of view and if we step outside the closed system we have created, our reality changes as well. For Mehemet the goddess of illusion, like the witch Mara in a story he narrates, is a seductress who persuades men that her reality alone is absolute. The characters in V. sacrifice their *virtu* on her altar. Yet in the soul of the goddess there is virtue. The lure of her body is great, for it is nothing other than relative outer life in its infinite variety, tattooed and fascinatingly colored. But man will continue to quest—or yo-yo—until he uncovers that inner fertility of awareness to which the goddess also gives access.

Chapter Three
A WOMAN IN THE WASTELAND

In *V.* the search for a unifying principle in history seems to fizzle out entropically. *The Crying of Lot 49* presents a heroine, Oedipa Maas, who is not only the most sympathetic and humane of all of Pynchon's characters, but is fully equal to the challenge of the quest for this principle. Rather than finding it in the image of an archetypal figure such as V., however, she finds it in a mysterious underground organization called Tristero. Cued to its existence by some enigmatic lines in a Jacobean revenge play, she undertakes both a scholarly search for the historical roots of Tristero and a California odyssey that includes a succession of encounters with very bizarre individuals. At last, having found Tristero's influence to be virtually omnipresent, and doubting her own sanity, she is admitted into what is presumably a secret Tristero meeting. But the reader never learns what Tristero really is, for at that point the novel ends.

At the outset, Oedipa is a bored California housewife, a Young Republican in analysis, who has just returned from a Tupperware party when she receives the call to adventure: a letter stating that she has been named co-executor to the estate of her ex-lover Pierce Inverarity, deceased corporate mogul. During his life Pierce was a "character," calling her up in the middle of the night and going through a number of vocal transformations, from secretary at the Transylvanian Consulate to comic-Negro to Pachuco to Gestapo officer to Lamont Cranston, as if he had no sane, comprehensible identity of his own.

For a husband, Oedipa has settled for the less colorful Mucho, a disc-jockey at KCUF, and a former used-car salesman who became depressed at the human and mechanical debris to which he was perpetually exposed. For him, pop radio is an escape from the horrible nothingness of the lot, but it is serenity bought at a price, for he does not believe in what he is doing. Furthermore, he does not believe in his marriage; he has affairs with teeny-boppers and fails to establish any sort of emotional communication with Oedipa. She asks Mucho's help in the matter of the will, but he evades the call. She must quest alone.

Oedipa is isolated, like the captive maiden Rapunzel, in the tower of her ego. She recalls a painting she and Pierce had once seen in Mexico: "in the central painting of a triptych. . .were a number of frail girls with heart-shaped faces, huge eyes, spun-gold hair, prisoners in the top room of a circular tower, embroidering a kind of tapestry which spilled out the slit windows and into a void, seeking hopelessly to fill the void: for all the other buildings and creatures, all the waves, ships and forests of the earth were contained in this tapestry, and the tapestry was the world" (p.10). In the events that follow, Oedipa attempts to fill the void "out there," spinning the Tristero conspiracy everywhere she looks, imposing a pattern on the universe—except that there is a strong possibility that Tristero is no mere manufactured conceit.

The first intimation of a pattern beneath the apparently random surface of Southern California reality is a vision Oedipa has as she drives into San Narciso, a conglomeration of shopping centers, tract houses, and industrial complexes built by Inverarity: "She looked down a slope, hoses which had grown up all together, like a well-tended crop, from the dull brown earth; and she thought of the time she'd opened a transistor radio to replace a battery and seen her first printed circuit. The ordered swirl of houses and streets, from this high angle, sprang at her now with the same unexpected, astonishing clarity as the circuit card had. Though she knew even less about radios than about Southern Californians, there were to both outward patterns a hieroglyphic sense of concealed meaning, of an intent to communicate. . . she and the Chevy seemed parked at the centre of an odd, religious instant" (p.13). This religious instant contains an inner, inexplicable meaning, a core of genuine transcendental experience. Oedipa's numinous insight contrasts with the stylized ecclesiastical movements of Mucho in his radio station, handling headsets and records as if they were chrism, censer, and chalice—trappings of a religion he does not believe in.

Oedipa gets a room at Echo Courts in San Narciso (the allusion is to Echo and Narcissus). The manager is a typical specimen of the California narcissist, a 16-year-old named Miles. He plays in a rock 'n' roll band called the Paranoids, who sport identical bangs and mohair suits and drooping jaws. Above the motel is a sheet-metal nymph bearing a remarkable resemblance to Oedipa. The implication is clear: Oedipa is an innocent, a contemporary plasticized Echo of conventional ideas. To qualify for the quest for Tristero, she must first be "sensitized," pierced by the incursion of a new level of experience. The lawyer Metzger, who is co-executor of the will, arrives the first night of her sojourn to fulfill that function. He himself lacks commitment: a former child-star in the movies ("Baby Igor") turned lawyer, he is interested enough in Oedipa to seduce her, but later in the book runs away from her—and the Inverarity case—with a 15-year-old girlfriend of one of the Paranoids.

In preparation for a game of Strip Botticelli with Metzger, Oedipa puts on multiple layers of clothing until she looks like "a beach ball with feet" (p.22), and it takes him twenty minutes to undress her. In similar fashion, Oedipa will have to strip away many layers of mystery during the course of her quest "before the Tristero could be revealed in its terrible nakedness" (p.36). Her first clues concern the strange symbol of a muted post horn and an underground mail service called WASTE.

While watching *The Courier's Tragedy*, a bloody revenge play by a minor

Jacobean dramatist, Richard Wharfinger, Oedipa encounters the word Tristero for the first time. The evil Angelo, Duke of Squamuglia, arranges to have his enemy Niccolo murdered by a group of men dressed in black, who are so feared by the other characters in the play that they are named only once:

> " 'No hallowed skein of stars can ward, I trow,
> Who's once been set his tryst with Trystero' " (p.52).

Later Oedipa discovers that these two lines are found only in a rare pirated edition of *The Courier's Tragedy* in the Vatican library, and in a suspicious paperback with a skull on the cover, published by an unknown company. She also learns that the "Trystero" lines were spoken only in the performance she witnessed; at all other performances, the conventional lines were substituted. Why?

She gets no answers from Randolph Driblette, director of the play, who asserts his right to take liberties with the text: " 'The words, who cares?. . . the reality is in *this* head. Mine. I'm the projector at the planetarium, all the closed little universe visible in the circle of the stage is coming out of my mouth, eyes, sometimes other orifices too' " (p.56). When the play closes down, so does Driblette's world. He cannot sustain the vision of a random world beyond his directorial control, so he takes a walk "into that vast sink of the primal blood of the Pacific" (p.122). But his metaphor stays with Oedipa: isn't it her duty, as an executor of Pierce's estate, to bring it "into pulsing stelliferous Meaning, all in a soaring dome around her" (p.58), by becoming a projector? Could she do it without becoming a solipsist like Driblette?

As Oedipa collects clues about Tristero, she often questions her sanity: she may be paranoid, imagining a pattern where none exists. The clues may have been planted by Inverarity; she may be the victim of an elaborate hoax. In this quest she is the only adventurer. The men in the book all resort to various escapist paths, protecting themselves from the frightening realizations she is making. But she doubts her own ability to complete the quest: "Oedipa wondered whether, at the end of this (if it were supposed to end), she too might not be left with only compiled memories of clues, announcements, intimations, but never the central truth itself, which must somehow each time be too bright for her memory to hold; which must always blaze out, destroying its own message irreversibly, leaving an overexposed blank when the ordinary world came back" (p.69). How can the finite mind, indeed, grasp and hold the infinite, even if it is able to glimpse it? For it is an ultimate wholeness, a universal order, that Oedipa seeks. The Tristero is her connection to that. Soon she is seeing the post horn, the sign of Tristero, everywhere. It is the emblem of the WASTE system, which most of the lost, alienated souls of this chaotic society are using in an attempt to have real communication with one another. The official channels of the U.S. Mail are not safe or appropriate for their deepest secrets.

On a night of drifting through the streets of San Francisco, Oedipa finds the post horn symbol tacked on a bulletin board in a laundromat, scratched on the back of a seat in a bus full of black workers, scrawled in chalk on the sidewalk for a children's jumprope game: "Decorating each alienation, each species of withdrawal, as cufflink, decal, aimless doodling, there was somehow always the post horn" (p.91). Are such clues, she wonders, "compensation. . .for having lost the direct, epileptic Word, the cry that might abolish the night" (p.87)?

The epileptic is said to remember only the signal announcing his seizure, "an odor, color, pure piercing grace not," a "secular announcement" (p.69), and not the revelation that comes with the attack. Oedipa may have to settle for the secular clues, the image of the post horn, the vague evidence of Tristero's omnipresence, and never pierce the coded, hieroglyphic pattern she saw in that "odd religious instant" above San Narciso to the concealed, sacred core.

The "Word" she is seeking is the same "stelliferous Meaning" for which Tristero and the post horn are only metaphors. The reality of the existence of the underground postal system WASTE and the Tristero conspiracy, founded in the Low Countries in the sixteenth century to oppose the established postal service, is not as important as what they symbolize. That Meaning is incommunicable; but, as Oedipa investigates the WASTE system (which is used by the alienated and the outcasts of society), she experiences some of the radical aloneness that her suburban middle-class tower had shielded her from. In the slums she comes across an old sailor suffering from delirium tremens, one of the numberless lost souls, with a post horn tattooed on his hand: "She was overcome all at once by a need to touch him, as if she could not believe in him, or would not remember him, without it. Exhausted, hardly knowing what she was doing, she came the last three steps and sat, took the man in her arms, actually held him, gazing out of her smudged eyes down the stairs, back into the morning. She felt wetness against her breast and saw that he was crying again. He hardly breathed but tears came as if being pumped. 'I can't help,' she whispered, rocking him, 'I can't help' " (p.93). She has spontaneously reached out to succor one of the lost souls created by the Protestant-capitalist tradition epitomized by Pierce Inverarity. She acts as the mother-goddess, bringing fertility back to the WASTE-land of modern life. And she rediscovers a part of herself among the have-nots—a group referred to in *Gravity's Rainbow* by the Calvinist term of preterite: the passed-over, the damned.

It was these outcasts that depressed Mucho so much back at the used car lot. He could not bear to face the nakedness of the universal human condition, his condition, of which their particular social condition reminded him. Poor people would come in a constant parade: ". . .bringing the most godawful of trade-ins: motorized, metal extensions of themselves, of their families and what their whole lives must be like, out there so naked for anybody, a stranger like himself, to look at. . .smelling hopelessly of children, supermarket booze, two, sometimes three generations of cigarette smokers, or only of dust. . ." (p.4). By the end of the novel Mucho has retreated far from the problem. He has begun the LSD therapy of Dr. Hilarius, Oedipa's psychiatrist, and the drug has dissolved his ego so that Oedipa feels she is talking to a roomful of people rather than a single individual. He sees an infinity of sameness everywhere—a triumph of entropy—and cannot tolerate dissonances (he even reacts to a slightly out-of-tune instrument in some Muzak). His sense of personal identity might be described as fragmented homogeneity: " 'Whenever I put the headset on now,' he'd continued, 'I really do understand what I find there. When those kids sing about "She loves you," yeah well, you know, she does, she's any number of people, all over the world, back through time, different colors, sizes, ages, shapes, distances from death, but she loves. And the "you" is everybody. And herself. Oedipa, the human voice, you know, it's a flipping miracle' " (p.106-107). Mucho is one of those who reject the quest that Oedipa alone has embraced. His acid nirvana is a false transcendence of the nagging problem of *waste*—the impure, unclean, anarchic element in human life.

Oedipa confronts the problem of waste within herself, as did Oedipus. At the beginning of the play *Oedipus Rex*, the city of Thebes has been laid waste by disease and crop failure. Oedipus launches a search for the individual who, as the gods have indicated, is the source of the pollution. That person turns out ironically to be himself. Oedipa harbors no hidden sin as he did, but she identifies with the preterite who, in the Puritan view, are the unregenerate sinners. Always she rejects drugs, which numb that compassion.

Dr. Hilarius eventually realizes that LSD is not the answer, for it dissolves individuality. He finds refuge instead in paranoia, and goes on a spree of shooting at imaginary Israelis from his office window. An ex-Nazi who, in concentration camps, experimented with inducing insanity by making faces too hideous to behold, Hilarius bears much guilt. For him Freudian therapy had been the means to tame the chaos, but it fails him, and chaos engulfs his own psyche. He responds by protecting a little paranoid corner of himself from the incursion rather than by committing spiritual suicide like Mucho or real suicide like Driblette.

Oedipa's paranoia is a holy disorder, unlike the doctor's. She is in the "orbiting ecstasy of a true paranoia" (p.137); like the traditional concept of epilepsy as a sacred disease, one that bestows religious insight on the sufferer, her paranoia gives her the ability to see order behind apparent randomness. And even if that order is only the malevolent shadow of Tristero—whose men in black capes, appearing in the counterfeit stamps used by the WASTE system, convey a decidedly sinister impression—it is nonetheless a force that unites the preterite, presaging the Counterforce of *Gravity's Rainbow*. It is the leading edge of "hierophany": a manifestation of sacred order, and possibly the only hope of rebirth for the wasteland of Pynchon's California.

As a true heroine, Oedipa is prepared to experience the transcendence that is an archetypal stage of the mythic quest. She is no longer the damsel locked in the tower waiting for rescue from without, weaving her tapestry of delusion to pass the time. She has become an agent for order, leaving the insularity of her home, venturing into dangerous, unknown regions, and attempting to bridge the world of appearances with the transcendent meaning that Tristero represents.

Oedipa is, in fact, a "sensitive." Although she fails the test for "sensitives" who can operate the Nefastis machine, a strange device that supposedly counteracts the Second Law of Thermodynamics, her sensitivity is proved in a later scene in which she accidentally finds herself in a convention of deaf-mutes. They dance to music in their heads, all of it different, and she is swung around the dance floor. She fears collisions, but none happen, because the deaf-mutes "hear" extrasensorily. They are sensitives, not relying on ordinary sense limitations, and she adapts well to their company.

The sensitive who operates the Nefastis machine supposedly contacts a tiny intelligence in the device known as Maxwell's Demon. The Demon, a concept actually used by the physicist James Clerk Maxwell, is an important motif in the novel. As it is explained to Oedipa: "The Demon could sit in a box among air molecules that were moving at all different random speeds, and sort out the fast molecules from the slow ones. Fast molecules have more energy than slow ones. Concentrate enough of them in one place and you have a region of high temperature. You can then use the difference in temperature between this hot region of the box and any cooler region, to drive a heat engine. Since the Demon only sat and sorted, you wouldn't have put any real work into the system. So you would be violating the Second Law of Thermodynamics, getting something for nothing, causing perpetual motion" (p.62). Without going into the complexities of the Nefastis machine which operates on this principle, it is possible to see the Demon in Oedipa at work as she sorts through the various clues she is presented with and comes out with energy in the form of greater information. Not really a have or a have-not, neither in the Establishment nor in Tristero, she can monitor the border line between the two and attempt to reduce the entropy of the whole system. By sorting the molecules—that is, by separating the world of appearances from the world Tristero represents—she learns of the existence of the alienated people of the world. The Second Law of Thermodynamics holds that entropy is inexorably increasing in the universe, but she circumvents that law and creates more orderliness through the information flow between her sorting Demon and her "sensitive" surface consciousness. This perpetual flow of information defies the Second Law; as in "Entropy," when human intelligence enters the thermodynamic equation, it is possible to reverse the trend toward greater disorder.

Maxwell's Demon is a version of the *daemon*, the intuitive intellect of man which often appears in Greek tragedy in the form of a powerful external force, a god (like Apollo in *Oedipus Rex*) who forces the hero towards an action that may have tragic consequences but is ultimately in the direction of life and growth. Oedipa listens to her Demon and thus has the only chance of anybody in the novel of resisting the entropic drift that is engulfing Mucho, Driblette, Hilarius, and Metzger like the relentless blood tide of the Pacific.

The main stumbling block to fulfillment of the quest for transcendence is the trap of narcissism in its various forms. To keep all one's love inside oneself, as the men in the book do, is to create a closed system, one that is highly susceptible to entropy. Only by keeping a channel of communication open to the outside—and to the lost, rejected parts of oneself—can creativity flow back and forth between oneself and others, between conscious and unconscious, and thus control the amount of disorder in the system. Oedipa achieves such a flow between her Demon and her conscious awareness, and she shares a flow of love with the drunken sailor and at the end with all the dispossessed of America.

Oedipa is uncertain by the end of the novel whether Tristero is part of Pierce's empire, whether he had left that too as part of his inheritance. Why did he possess a collection of stamps that included Tristero forgeries of conventional stamps? The issue is left unresolved, but she does realize that her quest to order Pierce's world has led her to the secret of the nation itself: "She had dedicated herself, weeks ago, to making sense of what Inverarity had left behind, never suspecting that the legacy was America" (p.134).

The real inheritors of the Inverarity empire are the disinherited anonymous American masses. Standing on a railroad track, she has an epiphany: she thinks of the kids, squatters, drifters who followed the tracks, sleeping in junkyards and freight cars, sharing a secret language "as if they were in exile from somewhere else invisible yet congruent with the cheered land she lived in" (p.135). And Tristero is the secret voice, muted like the post horn, but omnipresent, unmistakable.

In the final scene of the novel, Oedipa attends an auction of Pierce's Tristero forgeries, which have been designated as lot 49, and Loren Passerine, the finest auctioneer in the West, is "crying" the sale of these stamps: "The men inside the auction room wore black mohair and had pale, cruel faces. They watched her come in, trying each to conceal his thoughts. Loren Passerine, on his podium, hovered like a puppetmaster, his eyes bright, his smile practiced and relentless. He stared at her, smiling, as if saying, I'm surprised you actually came. . . . An assistant closed the heavy door on the lobby windows and the sun. She heard a lock snap shut; the sound

echoed a moment. Passerine spread his arms in a gesture that seemed to belong to the priesthood of some remote culture; perhaps to a descending angel. The auctioneer cleared his throat. Oedipa settled back, to await the crying of lot 49'' (p.138). It is futile to try to explain this ending, for the sense of ambiguity, of a mystery that is too bright (or too dark) for the mind to hold, is surely part of Pynchon's intention. But it is clear that a religious initiation rite of sorts is beginning; an apocalyptic vision awaits. Oedipa is about to pierce the mystery of Tristero and discover the truth that lies beneath its forbidding surface appearance. Certainly it is easy to fear the unknown; the auction scene reminds us of an advertisement Oedipa had seen in a latrine for the Almeda County Death Cult: "Once a month they were to choose some victim from among the innocent, the virtuous, the socially integrated and well-adjusted, using him sexually, then sacrificing him" (p.90). Does Loren Passerine have something equally horrible in mind for Oedipa? We are free to speculate, for the book ends with Oedipa on the verge of revelation; but if her inspirational epiphany is any indication, it is more likely that when Tristero's mysteries are revealed to her, Oedipa will not feel compelled, like Oedipus, to pluck out her eyes.

Tristero, in its "cruel" aspect, is like the sphinx that posed the riddle to Oedipus: "What walks on four legs in the morning, two legs in the afternoon, and three in the evening?" Oedipus's answer was "Man" (a baby crawls, an adult stands upright, an old man hobbles on a cane). This too is Oedipa's way of answering the riddle of Tristero. Her realization that the spirit of the American people is "coded" in Pierce Inverarity's testament shows that she has penetrated to the *human* level of the riddle.

Pynchon's evocation of Oedipus is purposeful. *Oedipus Rex*, like *Lot 49*, is a detective story, and it ends with the seeker reaching the final goal of his quest in himself. Oedipus's determination to find the culprit that was bringing the gods' disfavor upon Thebes resulted in the discovery of his incest and patricide. The play's theme is that the evil or good we see outside us is a reflection of the quality we harbor within. But Oedipa is a relative innocent; we need not expect a tragic ending. Her sensitivity has enabled her to detect Tristero, and her sympathy with the plight of the disinherited masses of the earth has entitled her to initiation.

The implication of the last scene of the novel is apocalyptic. Oedipa, about to be initiated into the mysteries of Tristero, watches the auctioneer gesture like a priest or a "descending angel." The angel that descends destroys, but destruction can have a creative context. Tristero signals the day of release for the preterite—that is, the alienated part of every human being, the part that has been damned to suffer in isolation, but has protected itself from worse kinds of insanity by its invisibility. Apocalypse means revelation, destruction of ignorance; and what is revealed when the last veil is rent is the order of pure consciousness, the Meaning behind the integrated circuitry of relative manifestation.

There is still no guarantee at the end that Tristero is real, that Oedipa is not imagining it. But the distinction between subjective and objective reality becomes unimportant at this point. The fact of her experience is real enough, and it is her changing consciousness that matters to the reader. Having realized the Meaning behind the Inverarity legacy of America—the common bond she shares with all people—she is spiritually reborn. And because it is a new order of spiritual reality she is entering, it makes little difference whether Tristero exists in actuality or in her mind.

To understand the full significance of Tristero's function in the novel we must introduce an important concept from Marc Edmund Jones's *Occult Philosophy*: the "profane mysteries." Jones is not a source for Pynchon but seems clearly relevant here. The profane mysteries are "the popularized form of occultism of any given age, often comprising untenable hypotheses which conceal but preserve a greater insight." The Tristero is the veil covering the sacred mysteries into which Oedipa is about to be initiated. She has had to penetrate the veil of malevolence which protects the esoteric and greater mysteries from those—such as Mucho, Metzger, Driblette, and Hilarius—who are not ready to receive them, and who are afraid of uncovering the inner regions of their own consciousness. The profane mysteries, with their absurd facade, repel many but serve as bridges for spiritual neophytes to greater realizations.

The profane mysteries are four in number, according to Jones: the ideas of the Avatar, of the Chosen People, of Prophecy, and of Signatures. Tristero appears as all of these.

The Avatar mystery holds that the lives of certain individuals (such as Jesus) provide an ideal pattern that should be recapitulated by any person seeking initiation. In the history of the Tristero organization there is the original founding father, Tristero himself, who felt himself dispossessed of his rightful inheritance to the office of Grand Master of the Post for the Low Countries, back in sixteenth century Brussels. "He styled himself El Desheredado, The Disinherited, and fashioned a livery of black for his followers, black to symbolize the only thing that truly belonged to them in their exile: the night" (p.120). Oedipa recapitulates the pattern of the original Tristero by discovering the Inverarity inheritance of the real America, of which she had been dispossessed, and by joining her sympathies to the preterite masses of lost souls who dwell on the shadowy fringes of society.

The mystery of the Chosen People indicates the idea of the spiritual fellowship of a certain group of people, such as the Jews. The lost Americans of the novel are the chosen people here, and in particular those in the inner circle of the Tristero organization which Oedipa seems to be entering at the end. They represent, in Jones's words, a "select company of advanced souls, an aristocracy of those with important if subjective lines of inheritance." That they have "pale, cruel faces" in *Lot 49* is certainly unsettling; perhaps

Pynchon puts no great trust in conventional images of spiritual advancement.

The mystery of Prophecy is the expression of apocalypse, "man's vision of the time when God assumes a full control of human destiny." The post horn is an image of the trumpet of apocalypse, and Oedipa's insights into the "hieratic geometry" underlying apparently random events is prophetic in that it pierces the notion that there is no higher order in the universe. Her whole detective quest is an attempt to read in the hieroglyphic of the world expressions of a higher purpose, and to align her destiny with it.

The mystery of Signatures is the idea that there exist "certain prophetic testimonies, guiding clues, intimations and suggestions found buried in written texts, preserved in representative objects or brought to focal significance from remote or generally inaccessible sources." The post horn is the key signature in the novel; the veiled references to Tristero in *The Courier's Tragedy* are also signatures, as are the subtle distortions of conventional postage stamps in the counterfeits used by WASTE. Oedipa's paranoia sensitizes her to these obscure clues to the underlying patterns of life.

If Tristero's superficial manifestations are the profane mysteries, what are the sacred mysteries into which Oedipa will be initiated? Pynchon does not develop this point; he leaves Oedipa on the verge of hearing the Word, but since that Word is inexpressible, he is better off suggesting it, planting it as a silent seed in our imaginations. He teases us. The story has been a quest to solve the mystery of Tristero, and at the end we are left hanging on the edge of its real meaning. Why does Pynchon withhold this most important element of information? It can only be that with the crying of lot 49 there occurs a quantum jump in levels of reality, from the profane to the sacred. Edward Mendelson, in "The Sacred, the Profane, and *The Crying of Lot 49*" (in *Pynchon: A Collection of Critical Essays*), says that the number 49 indicates the moment just before a Pentecostal revelation ("Pentecost" derives from the Greek for "fiftieth"): "This is why the novel ends with Oedipa waiting, with the 'true' nature of the Trystero never established: a manifestation of the sacred can only be believed in; it can never be proved beyond doubt." Pynchon's scope in the novel has been the profane world: its inmates, its losers, its intimations of a hidden sacred order. But that sacredness is a subjective experience. To expose it would be to render it profane. If he cannot express the inexpressible, he can at least suggest it.

The surface of phenomenal life is a constant ebb and flow; nothing lasts, especially in a superficial culture like Pynchon's California. To "go with the flow" in that tide is to commit spiritual suicide. The false absolute that Mucho and Driblette sought through sensationalism dissolved the boundaries of their egos in the infinitely changing world of sense perceptions. The conscious ego, for all its shortcomings, is at least a link with a greater consciousness, and this Oedipa senses. So she holds on to her individual ego and communes with the Demon, which leads her on her quest for greater wholeness of self based on non-change rather than change.

Pynchon challenges us all to wake our Demons and sort through the labyrinthine detail he gives us in this book. The more we read it, the less random it seems. Pynchon is as purposeful as James Joyce in his integration of every detail, every allusion, every word with a greater overall plan. The current of communication between his work and our minds reduces the entropy in both spheres.

The Crying of Lot 49 is a particular gem because it is brief, economical, and possesses a deceptively simple surface. Its essence is ambiguity, but the kind that expands the awareness, not befuddles it. Pynchon's achievement is to have embraced all contradictions: the novel is filled with topical allusions to contemporary culture that are at once trendy and mythic—and this mythic quality is found not only in such allusive names as "Oedipa" and "San Narciso," but in the whole pattern of the novel, in the eternal quest for transcendence.

Chapter Four
THE LOCUS OF TRANSFORMATION

The publication of *Gravity's Rainbow* in 1973 was a literary event of great moment. The book's epic proportions and striking orange jacket caught the eye; Pynchon's mystique and the critical controversy surrounding the novel accelerated its sales. But certainly many avid consumers of best-sellers must have been chagrined to find that this one required extraordinary concentration to understand and considerable tenaciousness to finish. Others, undeterred by its difficulty, discovered as fascinating and detailed a universe as had been created by any twentieth-century writer.

Gravity's Rainbow is a vision of incredible complexity, and no summary or analysis can do it justice. The central meaning of the book is apocalyptic; it is like a vivid flash in the reader's mind that cannot be sustained, an experience that cannot be reduced to a formulation. The best preparation for reading the novel is to read it; if we fall under Pynchon's spell, chances are we will never feel satisfied that we have finished it. Commentaries and criticism can aid understanding, but Pynchon has forged a pattern so intricate and charged with symbolic resonances that no mediating critic can fully put it together for us. The task of appreciation is quite upon the reader.

Why does one bother? Is it worth the travail? If we come to *Gravity's Rainbow* by way of *V.* and *The Crying of Lot 49* and have enjoyed Pynchon's sense of humor, his Byzantine thematic constructs, and his synthesizing grasp of large philosophical, scientific, psychological and social issues, then we have some idea of what to expect. But even that is not enough. The challenge of *Gravity's Rainbow* is on a different level than that of the first two books: greater demands are made, and greater rewards lie waiting.

V. presents a society in a drift towards entropy. In their various ways, the characters find themselves caught in a universal process of decay, and they have little ability to alter the course of their dissolution. The hothouse of intellectual analysis represented by Stencil turns out to be no alternative to the anti-intellectual chaos of the street represented by Profane: both men are caught equally in the jaws of V., the Death Mother. The redemptive power of the female is only hinted at in the novel.

In *The Crying of Lot 49*, Pynchon gives us a main character, Oedipa, who is both fully conscious of the entropic nature of the twentieth century wasteland and fully capable of positive action to find a meaning, a key, amidst the chaos. Her quest for Tristero goes further than Stencil's for V. because she has the capacity for sympathy with her fellow human beings that Stencil, in his abstracted intellect, lacks. What she discovers about Tristero is highly ambiguous, but we are left on the verge of revelation at the end.

In *Gravity's Rainbow*, the reader becomes chief quester, for the novel presents itself initially as a puzzle to be worked out. The main character, Tyrone Slothrop, an American lieutenant in Europe around the end of World War II, is searching for a mysterious rocket 00000, and for the secret of his relationship to this rocket that was implanted in his unconscious by a vast international conspiracy of corporations, politicians, and scientists known simply as "Them." We the readers must keep track of the conspiracy in its various manifestations, and decide to what extent, if any, it is a delusion.

The novel opens in London. British intelligence officials have learned that Slothrop has a unique talent: his erections occur at all the same points where German V-2 rockets later crash. He intrigues Pointsman, a Pavlovian psychologist whose ideas of stimulus and response appear to be jeopardized by this unexplainable power. It seems that as an infant, Slothrop had been conditioned by a scientist named Laszlo Jamf to respond to a mystery stimulus: in the presence of the "erectile plastic" Imipolex G, baby Tyrone would have an erection. Somehow the German rockets are triggering this conditioning once again.

Slothrop is transferred to the Riviera, where Katje Borgesius, Pointsman's agent, seduces him and ensures that he learns a great deal about the V-2 rocket. The purpose for this becomes clear later: Slothrop is intended to help "Them" sniff out the Schwarzkommando, a corps of Black rocket technicians, trained by the Germans and now gone underground to construct their own rocket. The Schwarzkommando are led by Oberst Enzian, who served under Blicero, a Nazi captain who supervised the firing of the mystery rocket 00000. Blicero's interests extended to more than rockets: Katje had been his sexual slave during a stint as double agent for the Allies.

Slothrop becomes convinced that Imipolex G, Laszlo Jamf, and something called the S-Gerat—which turns out to be the payload of rocket 00000—are connected with his destiny. Realizing that he is being watched by Them, Slothrop strikes out on his own to solve the mystery of his relationship with the rocket. The war has just ended and "the Zone"—Germany in the chaotic aftermath—is an open field for unpredictable adventures. He is chased by Major Marvy, a racist American officer who believes him to be a sympathizer with the Schwarzkommando. He is captured by Tchitcherine, a Russian who wants to kill Enzian, his half-brother, and who tries to use Slothrop to get to him. Slothrop plugs into a network of black-marketeers who provide him with false identities and dope. With inadvertent regularity he falls into bed with most of the female characters in the book, including Tchitcherine's girlfriend and witch Geli Tripping; former pornographic movie star Margherita Erdmann and her precocious pubescent daughter Bianca; and Leni Pokler, wife of Franz Pokler, who worked on Imipolex G under Blicero. The characters are all connected in various ways: for example, the conception of the Poklers' daughter Ilse was inspired by a film of a gang rape of Margherita during which Bianca had been conceived.

Slothrop's quest for the rocket 00000 is rather desultory. He strays further and further from his original purpose and finally disintegrates altogether as a character, disappearing from the narrative about 150 pages from the end. He does not die; he simply falls apart, as does the conventional logic of the story line. The development of an anarchic counterforce among former British intelligence agents coincides with an increase in the surrealism and fantasy of the narrative. Unlike most novels, this one does not become more coherent and more unified as the end approaches. Rather, it flies apart like a rocket explosion. Points of view fragment and drift away from each other, like separate "Zones" engaged in a literary diaspora. Even the reader, the ultimate center of unifying consciousness, is threatened with destruction at the end. Pynchon conveys an experience that defies our expectations and mocks the critic's attempt to reduce the novel's complex interweaving of motifs and ideas to a simple formula, as can be done with more assurance with *V.*

Gravity's Rainbow is not merely a code to crack, a "plot" perpetrated upon us by the author to tyrannize our analytical powers to the point of befuddlement; it is not a closed system, a linguistic box. It bursts the boundaries of its own literary structure and invites us to do the same with the limitations of our expectations. Herein lies its special reward. We can derive an experience from this book that makes us re-examine the whole structure of our experiencing apparatus.

To the same degree that Oedipa became a sorting demon in *The Crying of Lot 49,* we are challenged to become one for *Gravity's Rainbow.* The novel has no satisfactory central character to make the connections for us among the multitude of historical, scientific, literary, and other allusions, though the narrator gives us some help, as do Slothrop and many other characters who perceive conspiracies determining their lives. Aside from this lack of transparency in the novel's pattern is a major ambiguity in the novel's meaning: whether, in fact, the Great Conspiracy actually exists in the context of the novel; whether They are real. Many readers have assumed that the characters' paranoid preoccupations are an accurate description of their reality. But it is equally important to consider the alternative: as in *Lot 49*, the mind's tendency to see connections, patterns, and conspiracies may be a process of superimposition of an imaginary design upon a neutral situation. Pynchon proposes the state of "anti-paranoia, where nothing is connected to anything, a condition none of us can bear for long" (p.506). We must ask ourselves the question: can we be satisfied with the conspiracy theory, and if not, can we bear its alternative, that the universe is based on randomness, that there is no ordering intelligence behind events? As sorting demons we arrange elements to throw up a pattern against chaos, but how much objective reality does that pattern have? This is the central problem not only of reading *Gravity's Rainbow* but of living life. We must constantly compare our interpretation of reality with the actuality, and it is not always easy to see the "real" through our mental constructs. Reality changes sooner than our pictures of it, stored in memory, do.

Pynchon indicates that there is a synthesis between subjective and objective knowledge: this he calls the "interface," the crossroads of subject and object of perception, the locus of transformation from one state of consciousness to another. It is a boundary between opposites of many kinds and is itself beyond the boundaries of space and time. Here is the tightrope that anyone wishing to know the truth must walk. The reader teeters between his need for a consistent, completely reliable point of view within the novel and his utter inability to find one. Reality and fantasy are so blended that it becomes impossible to distinguish them: characters lose their sense of depth and become comic book constructions, or even disintegrate, as if the author no longer had any use for them; the insubstantial fabric of the artifice is exposed; plot summary becomes more and more futile as the novel, in the last 100 pages, seems to explode, losing what conventional narrative continuity it possessed.

To keep head above water amid the shifting levels of reality, the ambiguities, paradoxes, and oppositions of *Gravity's Rainbow*, we must imitate the author. Pynchon himself is a great tightrope walker. He has created a structure encompassing both perfect order and total randomness. Unpredictability of events characterized the two earlier novels as well, but here capriciousness knows no limits. Anything can happen. This is a delightful sensation for the reader, but entwined with the unpredictability is the justifiable impression that every detail, no matter how random it seems, falls into a grand pattern. The ordering intelligence of the author lends a certain gravity to his constant whimsical missiles.

For instance, at one point a group of drunken American soldiers, indulging in Pynchonian characters' penchant for breaking into song at odd moments, launch into a series of bawdy "rocket limericks" such as this one:

"There was a young fellow named Hector
Who was fond of a launcher-erector.
But the squishes and pops
Of acute pressure drops
Wrecked Hector's hydraulic connector" (p.356).

This seemingly carefree utterance has, in the context of the whole, somber overtones. The image of the V-2 rocket which dominates the book is associated with the sexual love of death in Western man, who has created a technology of awesome power; the rocket is a sexual symbol embodying the lust for flaming oblivion and escape from the insuperable tensions of life. The American soldiers, celebrating their conquest of the Germans, indicate that they share with the people they have conquered a similar obsession.

In Pynchon, everything is double-edged. The incessant satire has serious implications, and by the same token the "heavy" meanings of the book are tempered by the author's lighthearted spirit. Another instance of the tightrope: one cannot call Pynchon an optimist or a nihilist and have done with it. One mistake many critics have made, says Mark Siegel in *Pynchon: Creative Paranoia in 'Gravity's Rainbow'*, is that "each critical view has tended to isolate one of the relative points of view in the novel as an objective conception of Pynchon's point of view, while actually each point of view is really a part of an entire spectrum which is the 'rainbow' of possibilities encompassed by Pynchon's vision."

Gravity's Rainbow is first and foremost a satire, like Pynchon's other novels, but it includes tragedy, comedy, and romance as well. It is an encyclopedic anatomy of our civilization and attempts to leave nothing out. This very ambitiousness makes it inaccessible to many. The obscurity, the weight of allusions and cross-references, and the apparent chaos of the texture make it a difficult book to enter into initially. There is no room for the claustrophobic reader. We must make a space for ourselves, but once inside the novel we find that the strangeness of its landscape is no less unusual than the workings of our own mind. Pynchon's central opposition of paranoia and anti-paranoia becomes a problem we must solve for ourselves in order to make sense of the novel.

The two poles are contained in the image of the V-2 rocket's parabolic flight, a version of the recurrent rainbow. Human calculation and control determine the rocket's ascending flight; this is the paranoid phase, in which Their plan accounts for the rocket's position. Then, at the peak of the arc, the fuel cuts off, a point known as Brennschluss: "Ascending, programmed in a ritual of love. . .at Brennschluss it is done—the Rocket's purely feminine counterpart, the zero point at the center of the target, has submitted. All the rest will happen according to the laws of ballistics. The Rocket is helpless in it. Something else has taken over. Something beyond what was designed in" (p.260). When the fuel stops, so does the initial control, and Nature, or Gravity, takes over. It is responsible for the "anti-paranoia" phase of the arc. The rocket surrenders to the laws of nature which will carry it "plunging, burning, toward a terminal orgasm" (p.260), the culmination of a submission to entropy, to the natural drift to disorder.

This rainbow flight parallels the fortunes of Tyrone Slothrop. Slothrop spends the first half of the novel in his paranoid phase: he is manipulated by a behaviorist psychologist, Pointsman, who runs an experimental laboratory in England called "The White Visitation." Pointsman is trying to discover the cause behind the mysterious coincidence of Slothrop's sexual conquests at the precise places where V-2 rockets strike several days later. But Pointsman represents just the tip of the iceberg. The real force that controls and spies on Slothrop is a multinational cartel of corporations that owes no loyalty to any nation, but exists only to perpetuate its own power. The invisible "They" are the real villains behind Slothrop's predetermined destiny. About halfway through the novel, however, Slothrop enters his anti-paranoiac phase. He ceases to care about who is trying to control him or where he is going. Like a rocket plummeting towards destruction, he gives himself to gravity. He becomes harder to locate as a coherent character; he fragments, becomes reduced to a vague presence, represented by barely coherent memories and fantasies, and finally drops out of the story altogether. He has exploded, reached the "final Zero" point of the rocket's arc—the apocalyptic end.

The paranoia/anti-paranoia cycle is complicated by the fact that at any point, depending upon how we look at their situations, the characters are and are not controlled. It is rarely clear to what extent their paranoia is justified. As plots and conspiracies proliferate, it becomes more and more apparent that no one is really free from control himself, and this tends to negate the whole notion of control. Pointsman, for example, seems to be an important member of Them at first, but after he attempts to have Slothrop castrated and ends up with the wrong victim, a certain obnoxious American bigot Major Marvy, he loses power quickly. Several members of Pointsman's staff, Roger Mexico, "Pirate" Prentice, and Katje Borgesius, later become disaffected and join an abortive "Counterforce" movement to combat Them. Time after time, the manipulators, once we get to know them, are full of their own paranoid fears. The real powers, whoever They are, are never revealed. Even Walter Rathenau, supposedly the original "prophet and architect of the cartelized state," "a corporate Bismarck" (p.192) who established Big Business as a power greater than government, reveals through a medium after his death that compared to the real Powers on the Other Side, he knows very little. He asks the living, "Is it any use for me to tell you that all you believe is illusion?" (p.193). In other words, the belief of the controllers that they control is an illusion, because their own superiors control them— and so on indefinitely. The belief of the controlled in their predestination is also an illusion, because their lack of freedom is posited on the notion of their superiors' absolute freedom.

Freedom and control, when taken to extremes, turn into their opposites. The controller, theoretically free to manipulate, is enslaved by the nature of his relationship to that which he controls. The exploited, theoretically determined, can transcend their fate and find happiness in communion with others of the same fraternity.

In *Gravity's Rainbow*, the controllers are called the elect; in Calvinist theology, they are those who have been picked by God for salvation—and Calvinism is taken in this book as the representative philosophy for exploitative Western man regardless of nationality. Repressive governments, communist, fascist, or capitalist, all spring from that root. Those few with the power, the wealth, and the grace of God run the world; the rest, the preterite, have been "passed over" by God, damned to perdition, and simply are of no significance. The narrator of the novel is clearly in sympathy with this latter group. There are long catalogues of images of the forgotten people of the earth who emerge briefly from the background, vague and shadowy: "drunks, old veterans still in shock from ordnance 20 years obsolete, hustlers in city clothes, derelicts, exhausted women with more children than it seems could belong to anyone. . ." (p.3). They affect us, and certainly we identify with their side over the invisible Them, insofar as we admit this dichotomy as real. There is also the possibility, aside from being a member of Them or Us, of transcending it all by living on the "interface." We shall examine that concept later; first, we will take up the first of the terms that structure the novel: paranoia.

Paranoia constitutes the beginning of revelation in Pynchon's world, and is akin to a mystical vision: "It is nothing less than the onset, the leading edge, of the discovery that *everything is connected*, everything in the Creation, a secondary illumination—not yet blindingly One, but at least connected. . ." (p.820). All perception of order in the universe is thus *paranoia* in the etymological sense of being "beyond the mind"; that is, of being in an extra-rational frame of perception. The ultimate parlance, the God-term is *Them*: a plural way of saying Him. Scott Sanders, in "Pynchon's Paranoid History" (from *Mindful Pleasures*), has pointed out the many resemblances between the paranoid world-view and Calvinist theology. For example, the notion of a cosmic conspiracy translates in Calvinism to "God's plan," membership in the Firm (that is, being one of Them) to inclusion with the elect, and exclusion from the conspiracy to preterition. In other words, if we exalt to a metaphysical principle the notion that our lives are being controlled, God is the ultimate conspirator. He (or They) determines that we have no free will. This viewpoint is a kind of revelation in that it gives one a unified explanation of the way the universe works, a picture we can live with, however unhappily. Along with a glimpse of the cosmic order—which reassures—is the knowledge that we are cosmic victims—which depresses. For the paranoid has no privacy, no reference point in the self apart from his environment. He does not control his own life. Some vaguely malevolent deity or board of directors does. The paranoid mind, grasping for the comfort of a structure, entraps itself in a closed system.

Far from being an abnormal condition, paranoia in *Gravity's Rainbow* is the societal norm. The narrator himself is a paranoid, and he offers us plenty of evidence that there *is* a cosmic conspiracy. Walter Rathenau speaks from beyond the grave to advise a group representing Nazi corporate interests such as IG Farben. We are told that national allegiances have no claim on corporate owners: the real owners, through their giant cartels, create war and peace and even history itself. There is communication and cooperation between the living and dead elect. With immortality and ultimate power, They know no boundaries of nations and no boundaries of life and death.

The extent of Their control goes even to people's thoughts. Pirate Prentice, for instance, is one of Their agents, and he is useful because of his talent for living other people's fantasies. He is able to zero in on a person's obsessions and actually experience them. Thus he endures years of Lord Blatherard Osmo's fantasy about a giant adenoid that invades London, dissolving hapless troops in "a deluge of some disgusting orange mucus in which the unfortunate men are digested—not screaming but actually laughing, *enjoying* themselves. . ." (p.17). Pirate "pirates" Lord Osmo's vision, undergoing its horrors himself in order to set Osmo free to do the Firm's work. Control has become internal. The Elect cannot afford to feel fear if they are to do their work, so They Themselves are manipulated to blot out any thoughts that might interfere with Their ability to manipulate others.

Tyrone Slothrop has a particularly good reason to be paranoid. An American intelligence officer working in London in 1944, he marks with colored stars on a map of the city his frequent sexual conquests, accurately predicting in every case the fall of a V-2 rocket. He begins to think there exists a rocket with his name on it, and his friend Tantivy Mucker-Maffick assures him a little "operational paranoia" can be useful. You cannot hear the rocket, after all, until after it hits, as it travels faster than the speed of sound. There may be nothing but paranoia, which is extrasensory, beyond the mind, to warn you.

Slothrop's talent attracts the interest of Pointsman, who operates out of "The White Visitation," a partially-converted mental hospital devoted to the gathering of offbeat types of intelligence. Psychics, spiritualists, astrologers, as well as specialists in lobotomy, behaviorism, and statistical analysis inhabit the place. Pointsman feels threatened by Slothrop, whose prescient penis seems to give the lie to the cause-effect universe his science is based on. As a behavioral psychologist, Pointsman is a devotee of Pavlov and practices stimulus-response conditioning techniques on dogs. He cannot explain why the stimulus in Slothrop's case, the rocket, follows the response, the erection. He writes in his journal: "Whatever we find, there can be no doubt that he is, physiologically, historically, a monster. *We must never lose control.* The thought of him lost in the world of men, after the war, fills me with a deep dread I cannot extinguish" (p.169).

Slothrop gives Pointsman much to wonder about. Questioned under narcosis, Slothrop comes out with a memory of the Roseland Ballroom in Roxbury, Massachusetts. Slothrop was attending Harvard, and the Harvard boys at that time—including Jack Kennedy, we are told—would frequent the ballroom for its swing jazz. In a fantasy taking place in the men's room there, Slothrop imagines dropping his harmonica into the toilet and reaching inside to retrieve it. Threatened with buggery by the blacks who inhabit the ballroom, including young Malcolm X (who actually worked there in that period), Slothrop escapes down the toilet, where he discovers a whole world. The toilet harbors the preterite: "It is a place of sheltering from disaster" (p.77). He sees "shells of old, what seems to be fine-packed masonry ruins—weathered cell after cell, many of them roofless. Wood fires burn in black fireplaces, water simmers in rusty institutional-size lima-bean cans, and the steam goes up the leaky chimneys. And they sit about the worn flagstones, transacting some. . .he can't place it exactly. . . something vaguely religious. . ." (p.76).

Slothrop's fantasy reveals an essential characteristic of the white American psyche: a fear of blacks and an association of them with excrement, with waste. By association, Pynchon shows that the Calvinist temperament has always exploited and attempted to destroy what it fears. In the case of white America, it was the Blacks and Indians; in the case of the Germans, the Jews and the Hereros of Southwest Africa. Western man in general subjugates nature to serve him: rocks, trees, animals are the preterite to his elect dominance. There are, however, places of refuge where the preterite can commune with each other. The elect can try to flush away their fears, but in the depths of their unconscious minds the suppressed find sanctuary.

Slothrop unconsciously seems to share the typical Calvinist neurosis: the fear of the unknown, and the rejection as waste of all that is dark and threatening. Pointsman diagnoses him as a paranoid: "One bright, burning point, surrounded by darkness. Darkness it has, in a way, called up. Cut off, this bright point, perhaps to the end of the patient's life, from all other ideas, sensations, self-criticisms that might temper its flame, restore it to normalcy" (p.104). This psychological description of paranoia as an isolated consciousness surrounded by darkness fits most of the characters in the book—particularly Pointsman himself.

Pointsman rests his whole identity on a mechanistic model of the human will, that every action one chooses results from some conditioning. All life becomes binary: one or zero, action or non-action, depending on the presence of an appropriate stimulus. Following Pavlov, Pointsman imagines the cortex of the brain as composed of a multitude of off/on elements, like a computer. Each point has the capacity to be either active or dormant: there are no other possibilities. But Slothrop seems to have "spots of inertia" on his brain that do not respond to conditioning. Insofar as these isolated points of consciousness exist apart from the rest, as bright burning points surrounded by darkness, Slothrop is a paranoid. Pointsman's own paranoia of that which lies outside his control causes him to fear what he calls Slothrop's paranoia.

Slothrop threatens Pointsman's closed world view in which control is necessary to keep the darkness at a distance and to maintain his egoistic isolation. It is characteristic of all the elect in the novel that though they are theoretically in control of others, by entering into a deterministic frame they become infected with the paranoia of those they oppress. In the first part of the novel, Pointsman seems to be Slothrop's chief adversary. Pointsman sends him to the south of France; he has one of his spies, Katje Borgesius, take up with Slothrop, and also transfers Slothrop's friend Tantivy Mucker-Maffick to the front (and a speedy death) when it appears he is catching on to the conspiracy. But soon Slothrop eludes the net and escapes into the Zone, the area of demilitarized Germany immediately after the war, in which troops of several nationalities converge. On this interface, in this place which is, as it were, suspended in time, inside of a transcendent moment where improbability and unpredictability reign, Slothrop is able to escape Pointsman's control and surveillance. From this point on, Pointsman declines in importance, and we begin to see that in terms of the Cosmic Plot (if there is one), he is small fry.

The conspiracy against Slothrop began in 1920 when Dr. Laszlo Jamf performed some psychological experiments at Harvard. The scientist conditioned baby Tyrone to have an erection in the presence of Imipolex G, the "erectile plastic" later used in the construction of the V-2 rocket. Jamf deconditioned Slothrop, but not "beyond the Zero": that is, although the conditioning process was apparently reversed so that the stimulus no longer produced the erection, Jamf did not go far enough in extinguishing the reflex. Some vestige of the reflex persisted even when the stimulus was no longer present. Thus Slothrop's response to the rockets. Apparently Slothrop is a Zone unto himself, a field in which laws of cause and effect can be reversed, and response can precede stimulus.

This reversal threatens the elect's power structure, which is founded on the supposition that A can control B in a one-way manner. Man can exercise absolute power as long as he is active and the objective world remains passive. But as a voice from the Other Side babbles at one point through a medium: "The illusion of control. That A could do B. But that was false. Completely. No one can *do*. Things only happen, A and B are unreal, are names for parts that ought to be inseparable. . . ." (p.34). The spirit denies the secular religion of the elect that maintains absolute dichotomization through cause-effect analysis. When A and B interact relativistically in a holistic, give-and-take process, there can be no question of absolute control. The controller changes himself whenever he acts to change another.

The very notion of history dominant in the West encourages the irresponsible use of power and the illusion of control. This notion holds that all events are unique, not cyclic or archetypal. If we see time as linear, with a beginning and an apocalyptic end (like the arc of a rocket), and every event as an isolated occurrence, it becomes easy to exercise power without a sense of responsibility, as does a fantasy character Crutchfield, an American westwardman: "Not 'archetypical' westwardman, but *the only*. Understand, there was only one. There was only one Indian who ever fought him. Only one fight, one victory, one loss. And only one president, one assassin, and one election. True" (p.78). Crutchfield, as a member of the white elect, can exercise his sadistic sexual impulses on his Norwegian mulatto sidekick Whappo without any disturbing awareness that an action can come back on the doer, since once it is done, it is over. The elect can do what they want because there is only one "election." Solipsistically they assume that the one center of identity in themselves is the one valid reference point for interpreting events, and that other people are objects that may be acted upon with impunity because they also never change. (Pynchon's allusion to John Kennedy's assassination in the above quotation mocks the "one assassin" theory as the product of a paranoid imagination that reduces complex causes to a less fearful one-of-a-kind situation. This is not to say that its opposite, the "conspiracy" theory, is not also paranoid.)

According to the prophetic voice of Walter Rathenau, "All talk of cause and effect is secular history, and secular history is a diversionary tactic" (p.195). The War itself is seen as a great piece of theatre staged by Them to distract people from Their economic machinations. The violence and killing provide the raw material for secular history, but to the elect, who are in special favor with God, "the true war is a celebration of markets" (p.122). They buy and sell without regard for mere national boundaries, while holding out politics as part of the theatrical performance that diverts the preterite masses from the truth about Who really controls things.

From the paranoid standpoint, gravity's rainbow is a deterministic curve. The arc of history, with its finite structure, is inevitably drawn down to its apocalypse by the force of gravity. This poses a problem for the elect. The systems They control so carefully must succumb to entropy, because at a certain point the extrahuman force of gravity captures the soaring rocket of Their will and brings it back to earth, destroying it. As in Wagner's *Ring of the Nibelung*, the Gods find no safety in their Valhalla (which is connected to earth by a rainbow bridge); the repressed energies of the earth—in Wagner's cycle these are represented by the dwarf Albrecht—inexorably bring about Gotterdammerung.

To the paranoid—either elect or preterite—gravity's rainbow is a bad thing. It represents the closed circle of entropy and death. It threatens with extinction the precious isolation of the ego, of the little light of consciousness surrounded by darkness. Gravity makes sure that no one transcends the kingdom of death, even by rocket. Even the spirits on the Other Side gravitate back towards the world; they cannot seem to escape the gross world for the subtle heavenly regions.

The character that most clearly sees the nature of the problem is a German SS captain named Blicero (formerly Lieutenant Weissmann, who appeared in *V.*). Blicero oversees the firing of the super-rocket 00000 and attaches to it a hope that by doing so he can symbolically transcend the Kingdom of Death of which he himself is completely an agent. He has been regularly sodomizing a passive, golden-haired, blue-eyed youth (the perfect Aryan) named Gottfried, but he makes the supreme sacrifice: he stashes Gottfried, wrapped in an Imipolex G "shroud," into the rocket, as the "S-Gerat." Blicero, carried away by romantic Rilkean visions about the perfection of a life ended prematurely, experiences a kind of sexual ecstasy as he watches the boy's promise of escape "betrayed" to Gravity.

Blicero's very name signifies Death: "Blicker" was "the nickname the early Germans gave to Death. They saw him white: bleaching and blankness" (p.375). His original name, Weissmann, means "white man." Despite his abhorrence of what he represents and despite his desire to transcend it, he is nonetheless the victim of a controlling principle greater than his own will. To Gottfried he says: "I want to be taken in love: so taken that you and I, and death, and life, will be gathered, inseparable, into the radiance of what we would become. . . ." (p.844). Gottfried, whose name means "God's peace," represents Blicero's racial and sexual ideal, but because this ideal is so hopelessly perverted, the sacrifice goes for naught. Blicero, the chief villain in the book, becomes a tragically heroic figure in the best German romantic tradition.

Blicero's tyranny over Gottfried is one of many examples of the persistent paranoid idea that parents conspire against their own children. Blicero, a father-surrogate, sacrifices Gottfried in the "womb" of the rocket, the devouring mother. Slothrop's father sells out baby Tyrone to Laszlo Jamf in exchange for the boy's Harvard education. Pointsman lusts after children to be the objects of his Pavlovian experiments; their innocence stirs him sexually: "How seductively they lie ranked in their iron bedsteads, their virginal sheets, the darlings so artlessly erotic. . ." (p.57). And Margherita Erdmann, former pornographic film star, tortures her sexually precocious daughter Bianca, possibly to death. There are many references to mother conspiracies and father conspiracies. " 'Mother,' that's a civil-service category," says one character, "Mothers work for *Them*! They're the policemen of the soul. . ." (p.256). Blicero best expresses the paradoxical love-hate emotion that brings about parental betrayal: "Oh Gottfried of course yes you are beautiful to me but I'm dying. . .I want to get through it as honestly as I can, and your immortality rips at my heart—can't you see why I might want to destroy that, oh that *stupid clarity* in your eyes. . ." (p.844). Parents sacrifice, betray, and abuse their children out of an envious impulse to consume, orgiastically, the young and beautiful who seem to mock their dying and defeat. Tragically, when one generation tyrannizes the next, the young invariably become towards their children like the parents they hated. Gravity's rainbow triumphs again, keeping all beneath the overarching cycle of repetition and death.

The suspicion of the child that his parents plot against him is not yet the ultimate paranoia. Even closer to home is the idea that "The Man has a branch office in each of our brains, his corporate emblem is a white albatross, each local rep has a cover known as the Ego, and their mission in this world is Bad Shit" (p.831). The final extension of the conspiracy is our own egos, which usurp our total sense of identity and control the vast range of possible personalities that is contained within us. The albatross represents, perhaps, as for the Ancient Mariner, the sense of guilt which paralyzes our free will. We have only the illusion of control of our own lives; we are unconscious conspirators against ourselves.

The Firm's control seems omnipresent. *They* rule the regions of both life and death. They rig a facade of events called History to delude us with the doings of nations and armies while Their economic hegemony goes un-challenged. Technology, represented by the Rocket, is Their tool, and They use it unhesitatingly to destroy heretics. They can condition us without our knowledge using behaviorist techniques. They control our sexual responses, keep dossiers on us, and monitor all our activities. They have co-opted our own parents, playing on their sexual love of death. And They have even established outposts in our own heads: the tyrant Ego, the conscious sense of self, keeps a thumb on recalcitrant impulses that would change our per-sonalities in the direction of greater compassion towards our fellow preterite.

If a reader of *Gravity's Rainbow* wants to accept the paranoid world-view, the novelist will provide him plenty of evidence that the conspiracy really exists. Someone actually is chasing Slothrop all over Europe. Parents and parent-figures really do conspire against and abuse their children. The elect, in the form of various capitalist, colonialist, and exploitative enterprises, do exist, and the patterns of Their conquests do show remarkable resemblances. But it would be a mistake to conclude, as do some critics, that the novelist himself is a paranoid, that he actually believes in the monolithic conspiracy theory. Is not this "single assassin" mode of thinking another form of escape from the more complex reality? Perhaps there is no They, even though the novel's narrator seems to verify Their existence. The narrator's voice com-prises a number of relative viewpoints, some paranoid and some not. Mark Siegel says, "The apparently dualistic structures of the novel can be seen as structures of the narrator's mind. Each character can be taken. . .in the psychological sense of representing a single complex of thoughts and emotions in the mind of the narrator." Thus the narrator, seen through the characters that constitute the many facets of his mind, is as contradictory as any human being. Making absolute dichotomies is a characteristic of the paranoid mind, so for ourselves, if we want to accept the elect/preterite opposition, we had better see it only provisionally so as to keep our sanity.

To transcend the universe of the paranoid, the first step is to identify with the oppressed preterite, unite with our fellows as part of a counterforce that denies the absolute power of the elect. That will bring us to the second term that structures the novel: from paranoia we shift into anti-paranoia, the antithesis of the idea that reality is determined by the opposition of Them against Us. Anti-paranoia is represented by the downward half of the Rocket's arc, and instead of seeing conspiracy and control in every event, the anti-paranoid sees no connection between events whatsoever. He just doesn't care. He gives in to Gravity and allows it to pull him through a series of random occurrences towards the final, flaming end.

Halfway through the novel Slothrop finds that he has ceased to care about the mystery of the rocket 00000 and the Jamf/Imipolex connection to his past. He lets go of the "sanity" of paranoia that ties the universe into a neat package of set oppositions, and takes up the atheistic stance that there is no elect governing his destiny and pulling his preterite strings: "If there is something comforting—religious, if you want—about paranoia, there is still also anti-paranoia, where nothing is connected to anything, a condition not many of us can bear for long. Well right now Slothrop feels himself sliding onto the anti-paranoid part of his cycle, feels the whole city around him going back roofless, vulnerable, uncentered as he is, and only pasteboard images now of the Listening Enemy left between him and the wet sky. Either They have put him here for a reason, or he's just here. He isn't sure that he wouldn't, actually, rather have that *reason*. . . ." (p.506). His anti-paranoia results in "a general loss of emotion, a numbness he ought to be alarmed at" (p.572), but is not. The paranoid reality-construct seems now an illusion. He has entered a period of numbness and neutrality in which his very identity begins to disintegrate. He starts having trouble remembering where he is, and what he's doing, and why.

At the same time his adventures grow more outlandish. On the pleasure boat Anubis he is enticed into a relationship with the sadomasochistic Margherita Erdmann, and then with her nymphet daughter Bianca. But Bianca, who represents Slothrop's unattainable feminine ideal, is killed, and Slothrop's last connection to his stable paranoid identity is shattered: the hope of love departs, and with it the necessity of maintaining a conventional individuality. Slothrop continues to blunder through the Zone, and in the brightly-colored costume of a German Expressionist pig he takes part in a village celebration for "Plechazunga, the Pig Hero who, sometime back in the 10th century, routed a Viking invasion, appearing suddenly out of a thunderbolt and chasing a score of screaming Norsemen back into the sea" (p.661). Slothrop thus unwittingly assumes the role of preterite hero, a leader of the counterforce that will oppose the structured system of the elect with a chaotic burst of energy. Chased by MP's, Slothrop ends up in some baths where his arch-enemy Major Marvy is disporting himself with a Spanish beauty whose dark skin stimulates the racist American. In an ensuing raid, Marvy climbs into Slothrop's abandoned pig suit and is castrated in lieu of the lieutenant by Pointsman's men. Without even trying, Slothrop wreaks havoc upon the elect.

The patterns of paranoia and anti-paranoia are essentially mind-created. Each is what Pirate Prentice refers to as a "delusional system" (p.743). As long as we believe we are controlled, then we remain slaves; insofar as we conceptualize our freedom, we are able to act unrestricted by external control. As Slothrop runs wild, eluding the bureaucratic forces that have sought to suppress this dangerous, irrational factor, he spontaneously evades Their clutches by following his sense of anarchic fun. Other members of the Counterforce, such as Roger Mexico, catch the spirit late in the novel: Mexico breaks into a meeting of a high committee of the Establishment, leaps atop the conference table and urinates recklessly all over Them, "slashing up and down starched fronts, Phi Beta Kappa keys, Legions of Honour, Orders of Lenin, Iron Crosses, V.C.s, retirement watchchains, Dewey-for-President lapel pins. . ." (p.741)—the whole multinational conspiracy is ingloriously doused. Later, Mexico and Seaman Bodine (the same champion of gross laughter that appeared in *V.*) break up a formal dinner of corporate moguls. In their mealtime conversation they pour forth a catalogue of culinary catastrophes, all alliterative: snot soup, menstrual marmalade, bowel burgers, gangrene goulash, and many other equally disgusting dishes. The strategem succeeds, and one by one the diners exit gagging.

By the end, the Counterforce has come to include many who formerly worked for the elect. Chief among these is Oberst Enzian, a South West Africa Herero who was trained as a rocket specialist under Blicero and now has formed his own black rocket corps, the Schwarzkommando. They construct a replica of Blicero's rocket 00000—the rocket 00001—and this binary opposite of the original Nazi machine is the Counterforce's answer to the destructiveness inherent in the weapon. The two rockets symbolize opposing systems—one paranoid, the other anti-paranoid; the rocket of the Elect representing control and death, that of the preterite representing chaotic freedom. Ironically the Schwarzkommando also veer towards death: a certain faction among Enzian's men, the Empty Ones, wishes to commit mass suicide. Enzian, however, manages to thwart Ombindi, the leader of the Empty Ones. His own goal is life-affirming; he wishes to create for his tribe a condition transcending time: "The people will find the center again, the Center without time, the journey without hysteresis, where every departure is a return to the same place, the only place. . . ." (p.370). Instead of using the rocket as a means of murder or suicide, he wants it to be an instrument of liberation for the preterite Hereros, something that will propel them symbolically beyond the sphere of Gravity. It is not clear whether Enzian himself will be shot in the rocket 00001 like Gottfried was, and if so whether that heroic act will turn out to be, like Gottfried's, the illusion of transcendence and a vain sacrifice, or a true apotheosis. The issue is left hanging, as though the fate of the Counterforce (the counterculture? the Third World?) is yet to be decided in our own time.

Anti-paranoia is a false transcendence of the paranoid problem of control, and the anti-paranoid looks for escape from constraints through sex, drugs, and even death. Like the falling of the rocket "over its peak and down, plunging, burning, toward a terminal orgasm" (p.260), most of the characters in the novel at one time or another seek oblivion in sensual ecstasy—or agony. For example, Brigadier Pudding, head of The White Visitation, plunges into the pain of his memories of World War I, in which he lost most of his squadron through carelessness; he relives the bestiality of the battlefield through masochistic and coprophiliac orgies with Katje. To him, pain is "something real, something pure": it is "The clearest poetry, the endearment of greatest worth" (p.273). It helps obliterate the lies of scientists and politicians that he has for many years been party to. Although Pointsman uses Katje to gratify Pudding in order to keep him under his thumb, Pudding thinks he is escaping control, and after his death he becomes a full-fledged member of the Counterforce, even masterminding the infamous scatological sabotage of the corporate banquet.

Other anti-paranoids find temporary respite in their delusions of freedom. For the Argentine anarchist Squalidozzi, the Zone is an area of "openness," with unlimited potentialities for hope—and danger. It reminds him of "that first unscribbled serenity" of his native land, "that anarchic oneness of pampas and sky" (p.307). His political vision, however, runs into a dead end: he contracts Gerhardt von Goll to make a movie of *Martin Fierro*, an Argentine epic poem about an anarchist saint, but senses that the dream will be dismantled in its translation to the screen. For Margherita Erdmann, nihilistic sadomasochism is an attempt to penetrate to the serenity of Nothingness that she conceives as the primal unity of "the Center." But her "Sangraal" is "a heavy chalice of methyl methacrylate" (p.568); her torturers dress her in a costume of black polymer, stretch her on a plastic mattress, and ravish her with a gigantic Imipolex penis.

The anti-paranoid finds himself in the descending part of the Rocket's arc, as it were, and is confronted with certain destruction. His universe is winding down fast: the heat-death is around the corner, and to avoid thinking about the unthinkable, the apocalypse, he tries to loose the bonds of personal identity through impersonal sex; he tries on manic random behavior patterns; he bands together with others in a futile counterforce opposition to the Establishment. The anti-paranoid reaction is more appropriate to the

1960s and 1970s than the 1940s, and it is precisely Pynchon's intention to use World War II as a metaphor to describe contemporary culture. He sees the historical event as part of a cover-up that has been going on for millennia and which still continues: the war itself polarizes right and wrong according to the side we are on, but there is in truth no "enemy" but ourselves, and no innately evil adversary but our own ignorance of the innate universal basis of all existence. The novel as a whole affirms the unity of all men, elect and preterite alike, rather than the dichotomy of Them and Us which creates paranoia, or the anti-paranoid negation of the dichotomy which provides only temporary relief.

We must look beyond the polarity of paranoia and its antithesis, anti-paranoia, in order to sense Pynchon's overarching purpose. As Alan J. Friedman and Manfred Puetz have affirmed: "Pynchon's gigantic effort in *Gravity's Rainbow* can be seen as the effort of a writer who fully realizes the potentials of paranoid as well as antiparanoid delusions. His answer to the challenge of this dichotomy is the attempt to expose at once the dangers of both by showing that their respective ideals, structured order and entropic chaos, do not stand in final opposition to each other. If there is any single message cutting loud and clear through the infernal din of *Gravity's Rainbow*, it is the message that order and chaos (and hence paranoia and anti-paranoia) should not be seen as antagonists of the either/or type but as elements of one and the same universal movement. And without these elements there would be no such movement, no rainbow curve of existence, and no living universe for gravity to reign over." By refusing to accept either determinism or chaos as final, we can penetrate through the limitations of knowledge evinced by characters and narrator, and derive for ourselves a synthesis, of which ample indications are given in the text.

The resolution of the dilemma of whether the universe runs on pure determinacy (the paranoid vision) or chance (anti-paranoia) lies in Pynchon's use of film as a metaphorical and structural device. Not only does he make frequent allusions to films (particularly those by German director Fritz Lang), he structures the novel in frames of film. The sprockets between the sections indicate that each episode can be likened to a particular still shot, an undefinitive view of reality that will change in the very next frame. On one hand the film metaphor makes life seem totally determined, as inexorably set as the film going through the projector. On the other, we can all be filmmakers—and *are*, because our individual sensory machine is a recording camera that enables us to conceive a world as well as perceive one. Pynchon reminds us often that we are both in the film and out of it. He makes us identify with the preterite who are unwitting actors in Their film; he also enables us to transcend the linear time of the frame-by-frame, cause-effect structure of reality. It is possible to change that reality by becoming conscious of its form.

The dialectic of paranoia vs. anti-paranoia is resolved in the concept of "interface": the edge of transformation from one frame of film to the next. On that edge are contained all possibilities, and in that is our chance to seize the moment and change our reality if we want to. A quotation from Wernher von Braun begins the book: "Nature does not know extinction; all it knows is transformation. Everything science has taught me, and continues to teach me, strengthens my belief in the continuity of our spiritual existence after death." This comes from one of the fathers of the V-2 rocket, and as such von Braun represents the Firm, which wants to control life by turning it into death; yet the quotation is not merely ironic, as some critics have suggested. The deepest truth of the novel is that everything is alive and is energy. The Einsteinian implication that matter is a form of energy provides the bridge between life and death, between the known and the unknown.

The poet Rainer Maria Rilke is often mentioned in the novel, and though he was the hero of the agonized Blicero who used the poetry to confirm his desire for transcendence through pain, these lines from *Sonnets to Orpheus*, quoted in *Gravity's Rainbow*, indicate a holistic philosophy of transformation:

> "And though Earthliness forget you,
> To the stilled Earth say: I flow.
> To the rushing water speak: I am" (p.724).

Flow and Being coexist as do water and earth, and the human individuality says "I am" to the moving element and "I flow" to the element that is still. Humanity completes creation, providing either dynamism or stability where it is needed in order to fulfill Nature's plan. Man, despite his technology, does not stand outside Nature (or Gravity); he participates in it.

Gravity's Rainbow is not a polemic against technology, though it delineates technology's destructive potential for raping the human environment. The Great Serpent with its tail in its mouth, the dream image that inspired Kekule to discover the benzene ring, which led in turn to the aromatic chemical industry, is a key symbol for the natural power that man perverts toward selfish ends: "The Serpent that announces, 'The World is a closed thing, cyclical, resonant, eternally-returning,' is to be delivered into a system whose only aim is to *violate* the Cycle. Taking and not giving back, demanding that 'productivity' and 'earnings' keep on increasing with time, the System removing from the rest of the World these vast quantities of energy to keep its own tiny desperate fraction showing a profit: and not only most of humanity—most of the World, animal, vegetable and mineral, is laid waste in the process" (p.380). Technology, which harnesses the serpent power, is neutral in itself, but, just as intelligence can reduce entropy in the environment, so lack of intelligence can increase it. To understand the mythic roots of the serpent symbol, we must see it in connection with the ring of power from Wagner's *Ring of the Nibelung*, a major source for *Gravity's Rainbow*. In *Wagner's 'Ring' and Its Symbols*, Robert Donington comments that the

Ring symbolizes the higher self within each individual and the tremendous forces contained therein: "An extension of this is the famous *Uroboros* or tail-eater, a mythical serpent who creates, feeds on and transforms himself all in one magnificently continuous gesture, by swallowing his own tail. He stands both for the undifferentiated union of all the opposites in an unconscious state of nature, and for the highly differentiated union of opposites towards which it is the underlying purpose of the self to lead us through the increase of consciousness." The serpent power is Nature, then, and also the source of consciousness in man. He only perverts that power when he violates his deepest self by separating himself from Nature, by breaking the cycle that connects him to the world. The Ring can destroy the earth—or lead man back to "the highly differentiated union of opposites" that is the ultimate end of his striving. Technology can be redemptive if man can develop the level of conscious integration necessary to use it wisely.

Gravity, or Nature, leads man towards apocalypse, the Final Zero of the rocket's flight. This Zero would appear to be the flaming crash, but actually the Zero is everywhere. Every frame of reality is contingent to an interface in which time does not exist, and if we can stop the projector and experience that infinite moment, the deeper meaning of apocalypse—Revelation—will be apparent.

Pynchon uses his mathematical background to good advantage in suggesting the accessibility of revelation in human life. The apocalyptic moment is not the culmination of linear time, but may be located at any point of the Rocket's arc. The parabola in calculus can be divided into an infinite number of sections, each representing a certain change in time (delta-t). According to Zeno's paradox, the Rocket will never fall because a finer section of the parabola can always be found. As Lance W. Ozier explains in his essay "The Calculus of Transformation: More Mathematical Imagery in *Gravity's Rainbow*," when delta-t approaches the final zero point, the intervals between the sections become smaller and smaller, infinitely small, never arriving. Thus the rocket is always hanging over our heads, and this image simultaneously calls up anxiety and hope. It may fall on us or it may not. To get out of the closed cycle of linear time that the parabola describes, we can enter the interface between any two sections of it. Since the cycle of the Rocket, which inevitably ends in death, creates the trap of paranoid cause-effect thinking, each delta-t moment represents a doorway out of the closed circuit. Furthermore, the Brennschluss point at which the rocket ceases to fire turns out to be a type of this delta-t, indicating the transformation of the chronological into the eternal.

It is in terms of the concept of delta-t approaching zero that we must consider Slothrop's strange disintegration as a character toward the end of the novel. As the moment of delta-t becomes infinitesimally small, "the slices of time growing thinner and thinner, a succession of rooms with walls more silver, transparent, as the pure light of the zero comes nearer" (p.185),

Slothrop becomes less bound by time and space, and by the paranoid and anti-paranoid delusional systems that depend on temporal and spatial coordinates in consciousness. Slothrop becomes the Rocket, never to fall, always to remain an ultimate mystery. He can no longer be located because his reality is primarily subjective rather than objective. He does not die, yet he is "Scattered all over the Zone," which as a field of unpredictability is a great interface, a harbor for those who can escape the cycle.

Slothrop's scattering coincides with the Hiroshima atomic bomb blast, which occurred when Virgo was rising in the heavens (and Slothrop happens to be a double Virgo, astrologically), but his last experience as a coherent personality indicates his scattering is not a dying or a defeat. Lying "spread-eagled at his ease in the sun, at the edge of one of the ancient Plague towns he becomes a cross himself, a crossroads, a living intersection. . ." (p.728). Then, in an eternal moment, remembering the preterite detritus of civilization and feeling it embodied in his own life, he has a vision: "Slothrop sees a very thick rainbow here, a stout rainbow cock driven down out of pubic clouds into Earth, green wet valleyed Earth, and his chest fills and he stands crying, not a thing in his head, just feeling natural. . . (p.729)." Gravity's rainbow, which represented fatality and oppression to the paranoid mentality, becomes here a fertilizing symbol. Beholding it, Slothrop empties his mind of thoughts while remaining conscious (the "I am" of Rilke) and while emptying his heart of grief through tears (the "I flow"). Here the rainbow assumes its traditional significance as a manifest emblem of God's grace. In a book where God has appeared only as the repressive Them, the vague deterministic gods of paranoia, the most consistent religious presence is found in nature.

The rainbow is one version of the epiphany; others are intermittently found also in phenomena of light—dawn and sunset, the Kirghiz Light, the Brockengespenst, the Northern Lights, the Kalahari Light. In each case the light is a bath of rebirth. As the old wandering Kazakh singer, the aqyn, tells it:

> "The roar of Its voice is deafness,
> The flash of Its light is blindness.
> The floor of the desert rumbles,
> And Its face cannot be borne.
> And a man cannot be the same,
> After seeing the Kirghiz Light" (p.417).

This is the Center, the transcendence of time which Enzian seeks, and which he finds momentarily in his eventual meeting with his half-brother Tchitcherine. The two speak briefly, not knowing who each other is. In an equilibrium, black and white exchange a few words—not many, but enough to mark a reconciliation of spirits. Such a moment is the point of stillness that can be located through calculus everywhere on the Rocket's parabolic path; it is the glimmer of grace, the subtle kindness.

The interface also appears in the narrator's mention of the old idea of a Soniferous Aether, an invisible medium for sound that permeates all space. He postulates that "because of eddies in the Soniferous Aether, there will come to pass a very shallow pocket of no-sound. For a few seconds, in a particular place, nearly every night somewhere in the World, sound-energy from Outside is shut off. The roaring of the sun *stops* (p.810). The silence and stillness that underlie sound and motion occasionally break through—and experiencing these moments of "inertia," man becomes free of the limited ego, the Man's outpost in his brain, and starts to identify with the universal Self. The Aether is a medium of unification for the opposite phases of the paranoid/anti-paranoid cycle. Control and chaos, static immortality for the elect and suicide for the preterite—these alternating modes both result in destruction and entropy. "But an Aether sea to bear us world-to-world might bring us back a continuity, show us a kinder universe, more easygoing. . ." (p.847).

The Aether is everywhere, the interface is everywhere: all we have to do is stop the projector and have apocalypse now. the last scene of the novel takes place in the present. We readers are sitting in a theater in Los Angeles, watching a movie (of the novel? history? our own lives?) when suddenly the film breaks. The audience claps for the show to begin again; what they don't realize is that they are sitting on the interface of apocalypse. A rocket is descending on the theater: "And it is just here, just at this dark and silent frame, that the pointed tip of the Rocket, falling nearly a mile per second, absolutely and forever without sound, reaches its last unmeasurable gap above the roof of this old theatre, the last delta-t" (p.887). The awful moment just before the end has come. The meaning is ambiguous: is it the rocket Enzian or Blicero shot? Is it a third world war, a nuclear catastrophe? Or is it the leading edge of a radiant hour of enlightenment for mankind, of liberation from the cycle of entropy that we have been imprisoned in?

The author does not tell us, for the future is yet to be shaped by us all. As a hopeful invocation to the new age, however, he leads us in a hymn written by Slothrop's Puritan ancestor William:

> "There is a Hand to turn the time,
> Though thy Glass today be run,
> Till the Light that hath brought the Towers low
> Find the last poor Pret'rite one. . .
> Till the Riders sleep by ev'ry road,
> All through our crippl'd Zone,
> With a face on ev'ry mountainside,
> And a Soul in ev'ry stone. . . ." (p.887).

The sentiment, which parallels Blake's maxim "Everything that lives is holy," is an affirmation of the unity of all creation. Even stones have souls, and "we must also look to the untold, to the silence around us, to the passage of the next rock we notice" (p.714) in order to appreciate the full scope of history. All matter is energy: in that relativistic model, no preterite stone can be left unturned, or poor neglected preterite human being can be ignored, written off as "damned." The multiplicity of life is a continuity perpetually living, dying, and being recreated, and the individual consciousness is a frame in the great film that will flash instantaneously, plunge into silence, and flash again in a new form. Change is a constant, but there is also a constant principle, the "Hand to turn the time," that ensures a perpetual creative renewal and not merely an entropic winding-down of evolutionary energy.

Gravity's Rainbow is a true apocalyptic novel, and that implies not at all a story of the end of the world, but a prophetic vision of the end of human ignorance. We must keep in mind the signals of spiritual redemption in this book so dominated by perversion, entropy, and caustic irony. It goes a step beyond the preliminary explorations of *V.* and *The Crying of Lot 49*, and enters the deepest heart of darkness that can be remembered by our time. And there it exposes the radiance that can never be entirely obscured.

It is perhaps too easy to say that Pynchon's method leaves us with nothing but ambiguities. The "interface"—the synthesis of the concepts of determinism and randomness—is a tightrope strung above such logical distinctions. The reader continually walks it and is left hanging at the end, in that movie theater in L.A. He may be totally bewildered as to whether Pynchon is a nihilist or an optimist, or whether Slothrop is saved or damned at the end, or even whether *Gravity's Rainbow* is a profound masterpiece or a hollow literary fraud.

The novel's greatest ambiguity is the Rocket. It is Pynchon's all-purpose symbol. On one hand it represents the potential for human destructiveness; on the other, it is mankind's hope for redemption through technology. It even has a spiritual power, being compared at one point to the angels that announced the coming of Christ, at another to the Baby Jesus Himself. It has "charisma"—which, in the philosophy of Max Weber, whose writings Pynchon was familiar with, is a vital, original energy that manifests in individuals but tends to be co-opted and bureaucratized by the State. Thus the Rocket's creative potential becomes destructive when They turn its spiritual power towards Their selfish ends.

For the Hereros, the Zone's "scholar-magicians," the Rocket is a manifest symbol of spiritual power. They too try to bureaucratize its charisma. It is a holy "Text, to be picked to pieces, annotated, explicated, and masturbated until it's all squeezed limp of its last drop" (p.606). The Schwarzkommando organization inevitably grows more complex in its quest for this Text; Enzian's dream of primal unity gets more elusive. As the Hereros build rocket 00001, they literalize the Text while the "real Text" remains untouched, unmanifest, in the darkness beyond the Rocket.

The Rocket is also sexually ambiguous; it combines both male and female attributes. It is frequently described as phallic, as an assertion of manhood apart from the feminine darkness. But it is also Gottfried's "womb" and tomb, and the receiving end of a number of male sexual fantasies. It can also be a transcendent symbol uniting the opposites: rocket engineer Kurt Mondaugen sees "fuel and oxidizer as paired opposites, male and female principles uniting in the mystical egg of the combustion chamber: creation and destruction, fire and water, chemical plus and chemical minus" (p.469). Ultimately, then, the Rocket is androgynous, and as such represents a very ancient archetype—the androgyne. In her book *Androgyny*, June Singer elucidates the meaning of this symbol: "The idea of a Divine Androgyne is a consequence of the concept that Ultimate Being consists of a unity-totality. Within this unity-totality are seen to exist all the conjoined pairs of opposites at all levels of potentiality. Creation occurs when the cosmogonic egg is broken. Then the world is born. Or it occurs when male and female, having been incorporated in one spherical body, are separated by the supreme power of creation. Cosmic energy is generated by the surge of longing in each one of the two for the other." From his use of the "egg" symbol, Pynchon demonstrates his awareness of the mythic dimensions of the Rocket, and implies that its energy is cosmic and spiritual as well as physical. It assumes the status of a superhuman ideal of unity that the fragmented human beings in the novel attempt to approximate through love.

Though "we're strangers at the films, condemned to separate rows, aisles, exits, homegoings," there are "things to hold on to" (p.772)— a concept reminiscent of Rilke's emphasis in the *Duino Elegies* on the common everyday objects that ground us in a being beyond the separateness of our individual existence. Pynchon's descriptive catalogues convey his sense of the importance of the preterite, of the ordinary that we perpetually "pass over," in effecting spiritual transformation: "Far away in another corridor a loud drill-bit strains, smokes, just before snapping. Cafeteria trays and steelware rattle, an innocent and kind sound behind familiar regions of steam, fat at the edge of souring, cigarette smoke, washwater, disinfectant—a cafeteria in the middle of the day" (p.772). By opening themselves to the kindness that lives in such common perceptions, people can find channels of love between one another.

The relationship between Roger Mexico and Jessica Swanlake is a good example of how love between the sexes can transcend, in this case, the influence on Roger of Pointsman's "scientist-neutrality." Their communication is "mind-to-mind," and their union produces an inner awakening: "He'd seem himself a point on a moving wavefront, propagating through sterile history—a known past, a projectable future. But Jessica was the breaking of the wave. Suddenly there was a beach, the unpredictable. . .new life. . . . he might, with her, find his way to life and to joy" (p.146-147). Although this ecstasy is transitory, as it is so often in life, and Jessica goes back to her husband after the condition of crisis—the war that brought her and Roger together—ends, their union inspires one extended passage that is Pynchon's most impressive vision of the redemptive power of love.

Roger and Jessica stop by a church one Sunday evening before Christmas and hear vespers being sung. The description of the service blends into a remarkable catalogue of preterite sufferings and hopes. The War has stolen the essential life of the people: they are like so many used-up toothpaste tubes "emptied and returned to the War, heaps of dimly fragrant metal, phantoms of peppermint in the winter shacks" (p.152). Christmas, however, brings back hope for the children who used those toothpaste tubes, and for all of us: "There must have been evensong here long before the news of Christ. Surely for as long as there have been nights as bad as this one—something to raise the possibility of another night that could actually, with love and cock-crows, light the path home, banish the Adversary, destroy the boundaries between our lands, our bodies, our stories, all false, about who we are" (p.158). And this note of hope is sounded from the mouths of a makeshift choir of "exiles and horny kids, sullen civilians called up in their middle age, men fattening despite their hunger, flatulent because of it, pre-ulcerous, hoarse, runny-nosed, red-eyed, sore-throated, piss-swollen men suffering from acute lower backs and all day hangovers. . ." (p.159). But this igno-minious preterite groundswell of humanity still celebrates the vision of rebirth. Even those most miserably oppressed by the System, the War, or by their own deteriorating bodies, retain the hope of human fulfillment. This moment, filtered through the kindled perception of the lovers Roger and Jessica, is the novel's most sustained intimation of the immortality that can be gleaned in the most common moment, in the commonest of men.

Chapter Five
THE ROAD OF EXCESS

In *Gravity's Rainbow* the reader gets a heavy dose of harmonica and kazoo music, comic book characters, drugs, dreams, paranoia, the blues, sado-masochism, movies, anarchism, and pornography. These are means for Pynchon's characters to circumvent conventional reality, and the novel itself incorporates all of them into its form. William Blake said that the road of excess leads to the palace of wisdom, and Pynchon's art is predicated on this idea. Surely it is excessive that we must be put through the description of Brigadier Pudding's coprophiliac session with Katje, especially when all five senses are so vividly engaged. Here Pynchon's excess disgusts. Elsewhere the accretion of variations on a comic idea, repeated endlessly, leads to excessive hilarity. No better example of this can be found than "the Dis-gusting English Candy Drill," in which Slothrop forces down dozens of wine jellies—such as rhubarb creams, gin marshmallows, salted plums, marmalade surprises (with mayonnaise and orange peel)—in vain search for a digestible comestible.

Pynchon is one of those writers for whom nothing succeeds like excess. The question is: do we get to the palace of wisdom? Or, due to the author's love of ambiguity, are we left stranded in a wilderness of conjectures? David Leverenz has said of *Gravity's Rainbow*, "The story's undergraduate defenses against seriousness are themselves part of a more terrible seriousness." But we could as easily say that Pynchon's seriousness is only part of a greater laughter, the laughter of giants, of a Rabelais.

Pynchon operates in the satiric mode, where the line between comedy and tragedy is very tenuous. His novels belong to a kind of satire of which Northrop Frye explains "we must let go even of common sense as a standard. For common sense. . .has certain implied dogmas, notably that our customary associations with things form a solid basis for interpreting the present and predicting the future." Pynchon's excess makes us forget the standards of common sense and realize that all points of view are relative, and that our definitions and expectations concerning comedy and pathos are arbitrary. When, in *V.*, Esther Harwitz has her mystical experience during her nose job, "this delicious loss of Estherhood, becoming more and more a blob, with no worries, traumas, nothing: only Being," we may feel mingled emotions of amusement, superiority, sympathy, and possibly...belief. The commonsense moralist who judges from an independent frame of reference disappears in Pynchon. No judgment can be made that is not immediately qualified by its opposite.

The lack of a trustworthy frame of reference has brought Pynchon some criticism, of which this comment by Robert Alter on *Gravity's Rainbow* is a typical example: ". . .the unwillingness to make differential judgments about historical events results in a larger inadequacy of the novel as a whole. . . . One would never guess from this novel, for example, that there were after all significant differences between a totalitarianism unsurpassed in its ruthlessness and political systems that had some institutional guarantees of individual freedoms, or between a state that was dedicated to fulfillment through genocide and one that was not. . . ." In other words, "why aren't there any heroes and villains in *Gravity's Rainbow*? There were in the war itself. Why should Pynchon be able to get away with ignoring that fact?

Pynchon is not writing history. He uses history to construct a fantasy that has wholly other purposes than to reinforce conventional assumptions about how evil Hitler was. If we want evidence of Nazi sadism, we can find it in the novel, but it is in the context of a disease that has afflicted all of Western man for centuries. This disease is a schizophrenia, a compulsion to protect the ego against assaults from a dark, dangerous Other. It's Us against Them. All such dualisms are tentative: useful, perhaps, under certain circumstances, but never true for all people at all times.

The palace of wisdom Pynchon leads us to is a distrust for the conventional, commonsense way of looking at things, and a realization that our point of view is narrow, selective, prejudiced. It must be expanded beyond our present notions of reality. We must question their validity, even as we examine the assumptions of the narrator of *Gravity's Rainbow* with skepticism.

Pynchon is a writer for the age of the theory of relativity and the uncertainty principle. He makes the relativity of different frames of reference a literary as well as a scientific principle; he asserts the impossibility of absolute knowledge about relative phenomena. If there is an absolute, we must find it for ourselves, and toward that end Pynchon liberates us. At the end of the rainbow quest we all must make, Pynchon assures us that the walls of the palace of wisdom will ring with cosmic laughter.

BIBLIOGRAPHY

1. "Mortality and Mercy in Vienna," *Epoch*, Vol. 9 (Spring, 1959), p. 195-213.
2. "Low-Lands," *New World Writing*, Vol. 16 (1960), p. 85-108.
3. "Entropy," *Kenyon Review*, Vol. 22 (Spring, 1960), p. 277-292.
4. V. J. B. Lippincott, Philadelphia, 1963, Novel.
5. "The Secret Integration," *Saturday Evening Post*, Vol. 237 (Dec. 19-26, 1964), p. 36, 39, 42-44, 46-49, 51.
6. *The Crying of Lot 49*. J. P. Lippincott, Philadelphia, 1966, Novel.
7. "A Journey into the Mind of Watts," *New York Times Magazine*, June 12, 1966, p. 34-35, 78, 80-82, 84.
8. *Gravity's Rainbow*. Viking Press, New York, 1973, Novel.

SELECTED CRITICAL STUDIES

Alter, Robert. "The New American Novel," *Commentary*, Vol. 60 (November, 1975), p. 47-50.

Friedman, Alan J., and Manfred Puetz. "Science As Metaphor: Thomas Pynchon and *Gravity's Rainbow*," *Contemporary Literature*, Vol. 15 (1974), p. 345-359.

Levine, George, and David Leverenz, editors. *Mindful Pleasures: Essays on Thomas Pynchon*. Little, Brown, Boston, 1976, Anthology. Note especially the essays by Scott Sanders, Edward Mendelson, and David Leverenz.

Lippman, Bertram. "The Reader of Movies: Thomas Pynchon's *Gravity's Rainbow*," *University of Denver Quarterly*, Vol. 12 (1977), p. 1-46.

Mendelson, Edward, editor. *Pynchon: A Collection of Critical Essays*. Prentice-Hall, Englewood Cliffs, N. J., 1978, Anthology. Note especially the essays by Tony Tanner and Edward Mendelson.

Ozier, Lance W. "Antipointsman/Antimexico: Some Mathematical Imagery in *Gravity's Rainbow*," *Critique*, Vol. 16 (1974), p. 73-89.

Ozier, Lance W. "The Calculus of Transformation: More Mathematical Imagery in *Gravity's Rainbow*," *Twentieth Century Literature*, Vol. 21 (1975), p. 193-210.

Plater, William M. *The Grim Phoenix: Reconstructing Thomas Pynchon*. Indiana University Press, Bloomington, Indiana, 1978.

Siegel, Mark. *Pynchon: Creative Paranoia in 'Gravity's Rainbow'*. Kennikat Press, Port Washington, New York, 1978.

Slade, Joseph W. "Escaping Rationalization: Options for the Self in *Gravity's Rainbow*," *Critique*, Vol. 18 (1977), p. 27-38.

Slade, Joseph W. *Thomas Pynchon*. Warner Paperback Library, New York, 1974.

OTHER SOURCES

Adams, Henry. *The Education of Henry Adams: An Autobiography*. Houghton Mifflin, Boston, 1918.

Donington, Robert. *Wagner's 'Ring' and Its Symbols: The Music and the Myth*. St. Martin's Press, New York, 1974.

Frye, Northrop. *Anatomy of Criticism: Four Essays*. Princeton University Press, Princeton, N. J., 1957.

Jones, Marc Edmund. *Occult Philosophy*. Shambhala, Boulder, Colorado, 1977.

Neumann, Erich. *The Great Mother: An Analysis of the Archetype*. Princeton University Press, Princeton, N. J., 1963.

Singer, June. *Androgyny: Toward a New Theory of Sexuality*. Anchor/Doubleday, Garden City, New York, 1976.

THE MILFORD SERIES:
Popular Writers of Today
ISSN 0163-2469

1. *Robert A. Heinlein: Stranger in His Own Land*, by George Edgar Slusser.
2. *Alistair MacLean: The Key Is Fear*, by Robert A. Lee
3. *The Farthest Shores of Ursula K. Le Guin*, by George Edgar Slusser
4. *The Bradbury Chronicles*, by George Edgar Slusser
5. *John D. MacDonald & the Colorful World of Travis McGee*, F. Campbell
6. *Harlan Ellison: Unrepentant Harlequin*, by George Edgar Slusser
7. *Kurt Vonnegut: The Gospel from Outer Space*, by Clark Mayo
8. *The Space Odysseys of Arthur C. Clarke*, by George Edgar Slusser
9. *Aldiss Unbound: The Science Fiction of Brian Aldiss*, Richard Mathews
10. *The Delany Intersection : Samuel R. Delany*, by George Edgar Slusser
11. *The Classic Years of Robert A. Heinlein*, by George Edgar Slusser
12. *The Dream Quest of H. P. Lovecraft*, by Darrell Schweitzer
13. *Worlds Beyond the World: William Morris*, by Richard Mathews
15. *Lightning from a Clear Sky: J. R. R. Tolkien*, by Richard Mathews
17. *Conan's World and Robert E. Howard*, by Darrell Schweitzer
19. *Against Time's Arrow: Poul Anderson*, by Sandra Miesel
19. *The Clockwork Universe of Anthony Burgess*, by Richard Mathews
20. *The Haunted Man: David Lindsay*, by Colin Wilson
21. *Colin Wilson: The Outsider and Beyond*, by Clifford P. Bendau
22. *A Poetry of Force and Darkness: John Hawkes*, by Eliot Berry
23. *Science Fiction Voices #1*, edited by Darrell Schweitzer
24. *A Clash of Symbols: James Blish*, by Brian M. Stableford
25. *Science Fiction Voices #2*, edited by Jeffrey M. Elliot
26. *Earth Is the Alien Planet: J. G. Ballard*, by David Pringle
27. *Literary Voices #1*, edited by Jeffrey M. Elliot
28. *The Rainbow Quest of Thomas Pynchon*, by Douglas A. Mackey
29. *Science Fiction Voices #3*, edited by Jeffrey M. Elliot
30. *Still Worlds Collide: Philip Wylie*, by Clifford P. Bendau

All books $2.95 (Paper) and $8.95 (Cloth). To order, please send full price plus $1.00 postage and handling per order to The Borgo Press, P.O. Box 2845, San Bernardino, CA 92406, USA. California residents and libraries must add 6% sales tax. Write for our complete descriptive catalogue.